LOVE IS AN UPHILL T

'Some people write books and some books
write people. This one simply wrote itself, using
me, several pens and about eight cheap
exercise books. It turned out to be one of the
most pleasant jobs of my career.'

It is an open secret that many showbiz
personalities have their autobiographies
ghosted. But not Jimmy Savile. Here, written
in his own inimitable style, is the hilarious
story of his rise to fame. Frank, funny and
highly readable, it is a remarkable record of
struggle, determination and sheer exhilaration.
And it's a real pleasure to read.

Love is an Uphill Thing

Previously published as
As it Happens

Jimmy Savile O.B.E

CORONET BOOKS
Hodder and Stoughton

First published in Great Britain in 1974 by Barrie and
Jenkins Limited under the title *As it Happens*

Coronet edition 1976

Printed and bound in Great Britain
for Coronet Books,
Hodder and Stoughton,
London
by Hazell Watson & Viney Ltd,
Aylesbury, Bucks

ISBN 0 340 19925 3

To all my wonderful friends. Be they of a day, a night or lifelong. Speed the hours that we may all join up again in Heaven.

P.S. As it happens, that means you too, if you don't mind!

Love is an Uphill Thing

CHAPTER ONE

'Don't call us, we'll call you' is the famous showbiz brushoff. I claim to be the youngest recipient of this award, at the age of two, and from the Big Agent Himself, the Good Lord!

Actually at not quite two years old I was dying. The Master, or one of his minders, hearing of this imminent addition to his heavenly host, sent in the nick of time a miracle cure.

After some years of a strange life and several occasions when I could have quite easily died, and nearly did, it gradually dawned on me that the Good Lord is as determined not to have me join his heavenly army as I am apparently determined to enlist.

Some babies are born strong, some weak. Being the youngest of seven it would appear that my father's last effort was lacking in the juices of strength. Eye-witnesses have it that I was born sound asleep.

Much love and care sustained my shrimplike form until finally, anointed with the oils of the last rites and resembling one of Mr Skipper's excellent sardines, my maternal grandma lowered a mirror over my mouth to catch the bloom of the last breath. My mama, who was to become famous as 'the Duchess' and my only real true love to date, was in Leeds Cathedral offering a prayer of intercession to a then unknown, but hopefully possible saint, Margaret Sinclair. At that precise moment my grandma collected not the last breath but a right eyeful of involuntary, well aimed pee.

I have continued to pee on the Establishment ever since with similar success.

Letters of confirmation from astounded doctors, nurses and priests are even now lodged in the Vatican and have played their part in the long process of beatification of Margaret Sinclair who is now a 'Blessed', which in saintly terms makes her a sort of corporal, before a commission.

Having got over the imminent danger of my obviously unwelcome arrival at the Golden Gates the Good Lord busied Himself with other matters and left me in such a state that at fourteen I still qualified for free malt at school. To be a jockey was a natural for a five-stone teenager but it was obvious that to straddle even the most knackered of horses would split me asunder. It was all I could do to accommodate a bicycle saddle.

Heartened by my urinary success of catching my grandmother fair and square I continued in my infancy to pee on anything or anyone who unwarily came into range, and my first recorded applauses were for direct hits on guests, fires, teatables, priests and other such targets.

I wasn't very popular for a number of years.

Another of my stumbling blocks on the road to being universally loved was lack of tact. As a family we were quite poor and a lot of our relatives were quite wealthy. Remarks like 'My mam says it didn't cost that much' brought expert backhanders from the Duchess, so my early life was marked by a sensible silence and big ears.

I mourn the passing of those factories of learning called 'elementary schools'. I joined the one known as St Anne's, in Leeds, at four and stayed till my fourteenth birthday. No exams were there to bother us. Each year we all moved up into the next class—except for some scholars who disappeared backwards into 'special schools'. Most pupils distinguished themselves in later life. At least two got hanged, several are self-made millionaires, I won forty No 1 awards for various showbiz successes, and there was one very polite pupil with a gorgeous sister, who went into films and has done O.K. His name was, and still is, Peter O'Toole.

In those days corporal punishment was the norm. At my

school it was a short bamboo cane across the open hand delivered by the headmaster. While it never stopped the bad boys being bad it had a salutory effect on the rest of us and the only true silence in the class was when the Head's door opened and a weeping rebel emerged. A shiver of apprehension would run through us all. Advocates of 'one of the best' on each hand can be sure that at least ninety-eight per cent of our robust pupils were kept in order by its very prospect.

I got my very first taste of a Borstal at the age of nine. Not as a guest but a visitor. Both my parents were great social workers and were invited to visit our local offenders' school and took me along. Stern were the warnings of the Duchess on the unlikely event of me gaining enough strength to be a wrongdoer. Unfortunately my only impressions were of well kept gardens and enormous trays of fruitcake in the Borstal bakehouse. Compared to the living arrangements of the vast majority of my school-fellows I felt that the Borstal lads had quite a lot going for them.

Consuming my daily spoonful of free, sticky malt and quarter pint of milk I soldiered on, on the touchlines of life, and when Hitler raped the Low Countries someone tied a great luggage label round my neck and evacuated me to Gainsborough in Lincolnshire. I loved it. From the black streets of Leeds to a place where trees grew near houses. Smells of grass and early morning woodsmoke replaced soot and sodium. We foreign schoolkids were set to sandbagging local buildings of importance. My first taste of manual labour was, naturally, holding the neck of the bag open. After six months of heavenly new sights and sounds my folks came over and, finding me billeted near several large tanks of gasolene, decided I might as well get blown up in Leeds as fried in Gainsborough. So it was back home to a strange, blacked-out city and my first tastes of a new dimension in which I was to be a world champion.

11

The Dance Hall.

To be eleven years old and have the complete free run of the main dance hall of a wartime city that was headlined by one Sunday paper as 'The City of Sin' gave me an education that qualified me for every A level that ever existed in Hell.

Not yet five feet in height, as thin as a drumstick, with big eyes, ears and nose, I was everyone's mascot, pet, runner, holder of mysterious parcels and secrets. Because I didn't understand the first thing about anything I was the confidant of murderers, whores, black marketeers, crooks of every trade—and often of the innocent victims they preyed on. I also played the drums.

With the war machine eating up all the young men, the dance hall employed a ladies' five-piece band. From seven till eleven they played six nights a week. The dance hall manager—an incredible, genial, fiddling rogue—drew £50 a week for a relief band for the half-hour interval. In actual fact I was the relief band and got 10s. a week. The pianist was one of the band girls who just took her own break when she could. The two of us had quite a job to be heard over the noise of a thousand dancers, all the men wearing heavy boots, but afternoon and evening we thumped it out. Being hopelessly under age and therefore highly illegal there were times when I was persona non grata on stage. 'Don't come in tomorrow,' the manager would hiss. 'The directors are coming.' When the visiting boss asked, 'Where's the second band?' the suave reply never failed: 'There's a big air raid going on in Hull [or Doncaster or Halifax] and the relief band is made up of firemen.' There were always lots of fires but lots of 10s. for me. School would be over by 4 p.m. and at ten past I'd be on stage playing for the afternoon session.

Night times were a dream. When the sirens sounded I'd go up on the roof and hasten down with messages of impending local fires. After the session I would be under the seats looking for full packets of cigarettes and, when the Yanks hit

12

town, full packs of 200. These I would give to the night-watchman and at that age would never think of keeping the precious-as-gold finds for myself. What excitement this never-ending war was. At the time of Dunkirk (not that I even knew where it was), the area round Leeds station was full of exhausted troops sleeping on the pavements in broad daylight until billets were found for them.

A stick of bombs that fell near our house blew up several of our neighbours and caused other friends to move in with us temporarily. The Duchess used to play war songs on the piano and a great time was had by all.

Years later, after she had moved to my film-star flat on the seafront at Scarborough, I did some great detective work and found fifteen of her original gang. They were smuggled into the old house, the Duchess was ordered to Leeds on some pretext, and as she walked in and switched the lights on, lo, back turned the clock thirty years and the old faces were there for yet another party. Many were the tears, the songs and the memories.

Of such nights is the good life made.

At the age of twelve I had my first date with a real girl. She was about twenty and worked in the dance hall cashbox. As I only ever saw the top ten per cent of her through the glass it never occurred to me that there was a bottom bit. I used to get tickets for daytime cinema trade shows but couldn't go on my own being too young and too small. She was mightily standoffish and wouldn't tolerate the local civilian bootleggers. I was obviously of much safer stuff and was the envy of all. The night before the big day personal disaster struck and in the perpetual blackout I walked into some iron railings and bust my top lip open. The darkness of the picture house hid my floppy lip and I discovered about girls that 90 percent you can't see is just as important as the 10 per cent you can. These days the percentage is reversed but the principle is the same.

A time of great excitement for me was when one of our lady patrons was discovered in several carrier bags in a ditch. Murder they called it, and it was a whole new scene to me. I could never work out why it was necessary to cut her into bits. It was all part of a strange adult world that I never tried to understand, and even though I had a good idea who'd done it, no one ever asked me. Besides, I was far too excited about leaving school the following month.

And so it passed. At fourteen I was outside with only the most pleasant memories of my official educational process plus a world of wisdom from my after-hours way of life. The war was still at its height, there was nothing of anything, but life was good because of its very simplicity. My parents' working instructions were simple. 'Whatever job you take you must keep for at least one year.'

I went into an office as a junior only because I would wear a suit. With five years of dance hall life behind me it was inconceivable that I could ever don overalls. I didn't know anything about machines but I knew everything about people.

The office didn't really know what hit them. It's not every day the office boy of fourteen is far more adult than the rest of the staff put together. Dutifully for a year I laboured from 8.30 till 6 for the sum of 13s. 9d. a week. Actually it was 15s. less stoppages. My pockets were always full of money. Though it didn't interest me in the least, even at that age I developed a Midas touch.

My first year's contribution to the economy was high-lighted by a shattering explosion which nearly blew the office and its toilers into the next street. It was all to do with the gas central heating. During an air raid warning the night before, I had been on all-night firewatch duty and turned off the necessary main taps. The youth who re-ignited the con-traption got the taps mixed up and upon applying the naked flame had received a blast of atomic proportions. Hurling him bodily from the boiler house, the ensuing reaction ran amok through the pipes and blew up desks, doors, walls and sprayed the startled occupants with dank water which had been circulating for twenty years. Even then my Midas touch was evident, for did it not blow open a room that had been hidden for years and reveal a considerable stock of shoe-making equipment. Precious, in those days, it was sold for far more than the damage cost.

Having to move on to work of more national importance and waiting for the inevitable call-up I moved into a large concern which handled vital foodstuffs. Quantities of these foodstuffs, particularly currants, raisins and suchlike, I con-sidered vital to my own economy and if some of my pockets carried money, the others carried pounds of dried fruits. Not that I stole them—far from it. They came from boxes which had burst. (But I *had* dropped the boxes in the first place!)

During the lunch hour at this new job some staff played cards. My earlier after-school activities had made me pro-ficient in dealing—from the top, bottom or even middle of the deck. It never occurred to me to take from the other players, just as crooked but not nearly as good, any more than I might need for the evening's enjoyment or to subsidize a penniless friend. A few shillings for the pictures was enough.

The fact that I've never been greedy could be the reason I've never been to jail.

Several of my evenings at this time were taken up with the intricacies of the morse code, aircraft recognition, and being lead drummer of the A.T.C.'s 168 squadron. My distinction in this noble body of embryo airmen was to be the longest serving cadet without one qualification of any sort. In itself a considerable achievement. When stripes and badges were handed out I was an automatic non-starter. If you are small it's easier to make general than corporal.

Having survived on the touchlines of life for so long, the

15

fates dealt me several good hands. The first was a bicycle. Without a doubt my passport to health and strength, a bike was my constant companion and saviour—and is even to this day. In those days there were no cars on the roads, no motorways and the whole country was a giant fairy kingdom. A week's holiday would see me off on my own round Scotland and I would cover well over 1,000 miles. Finding undiscovered strengths turned me into a racing cyclist of international ability, but still dogged by a strange easy-going nature. In one important race two of us were well in the lead. With only five miles to the finish we came across two girls having a picnic by the roadside. In a twinkling we were off the bikes, on the rug, and as our competitors sped by we raised the girls' flasks on high in salute.

The Tour of Britain is a bike race of world class. I was riding for the North of England team in the very first one. At all the stage towns the riders were treated like pop stars, and the girls would flock round. But in those days athletes were made of stern stuff and were usually in bed by 10 p.m.

All except me. Fittened by the day's gruelling race and fed well by the sponsors (in that year the *Daily Express*), by 10 p.m. I was raring to go, but not to sleep. With romance aplenty at every finishing stage and crawling to bed at 3 a.m., I held on grimly to my usual position—last. On the stage from Morecambe to Glasgow it poured with rain. One of the riders came alongside and pointed out that his finances were at a low ebb. He needed to win some cash that day but would find it difficult to build up sufficient lead. If, he pointed out further, I was to make a break from the leading bunch and he pretended to chase me, this would be such a joke that no one would take it seriously and he could make his own escape once we were out of sight.

I slipped into top gear and flashed past a surprised bunch at 40 m.p.h. Everyone cheered like mad and dissolved with laughter. My pal in the plot, a London barrowboy in his business capacity, set up a great comic to-do pretending to chase my fleeing form. Once out of sight we settled down to some hard work. At Kendal we were seven minutes in the lead. Climbing the notorious Shap Fell outside the town, he forged ahead to take the £10 prize for the first over the summit, thereby restoring his finances, and I paid the penalty for my particular brand of late-night training. At the bottom of that cruel hill I was in the lead, at the top I was my usual last! At that moment the fates decided to give my future yet another incredible twist.

First of all a car following the race offered me a lift before I dropped dead like the celebrated Black Bess. This put me out of the race but the *Daily Express* were loth to let me go because in those days athletes who were sparky characters were the exception rather than the rule. On a brainwave the organizer sent for another loudspeaker car and asked me to do part of the race commentary. It turned out that I was a natural ad-lib broadcaster and finished up entertaining crowds up to 50,000 without turning a hair.

This lurking ability sealed my racing fate. My chat was far more valuable than my legs.

From shrimp to champ, the bike gave me too much to ever leave the game. As recently as 1973 I did the 1,000 mile run from Land's End to John o' Groat's. It's an outside way of life which is quite incomparable.

CHAPTER TWO

The war was by now consuming humans at an awesome rate. The flower of British manhood had been harvested and the authorities were obviously starting on the stalks and roots because they passed me A1. The question was, what to join. My heroes at the time were my two older brothers, John and Vince. Both were in the Navy, but I couldn't swim so that was out. Being still a lightweight it was obvious that to don the boots of the army would keep me almost permanently welded to the floor. That anyone should add sixty pounds of equipment to my frame I would, like Lot's wife, be stilled for ever.

There was at the time a marked shortage of rear gunners for the R.A.F. Their job carried a high, four to one, ratio of finishing up in heaven instead of back in the NAAFI. I still fancied the job but on investigation the R.A.F. explained that one of the basic requirements was that the gunner-to-be should be able to see the enemy. My eyes appeared to be in a class of their own. They, the R.A.F., felt that I could be of more use to the British war effort if I was loaned to the enemy.

In the midst of all these high-power decisions, Mr Ernest Bevin, the Minister of Labour, made his bi-annual lottery draw and I was told to report to the coalmines. While not exactly forced labour, if you didn't do it you went to jail.

The method of selecting men for the mines was simple. Numbers from 1 to zero were put in a hat or some such ministerial receptacle and Mr Bevin drew out one. All conscripts whose national service number ended with that particular digit were destined for the big drop. That was one man in ten, right across the board.

Startled miners had to deal with a sudden influx of the most incredible and bizarre types. Among my batch were doctors, auctioneers, farmers, officer cadets, clerks and—most startled of all—me!

My introduction to the delights of the earth's bowels was simple. 'All aboard the cage lads' boomed a cheery onsetter, and then 2,000 feet worth of WHOOSH! Twenty-five white, wobbly-legged flower of British youth emerged like cattle to the abattoir. Close together for moral support and just the occasional bleat.

First impressions can be important. Mine were threefold. Within the first ten minutes I had tripped over a rail, narrowly escaped being run over by a Walt Disney-size coal wagon and, trying to find a less lethal spot in this dark and clanking world, dashed my brains against a steel roof support.

It was soon apparent to the authorities that to teach the average Bevin boy to win coal from its seventy-million-year resting place would take almost as long. Their time and patience was totally consumed by preventing us getting crushed, squashed, maimed or decapitated before they could allocate us to some unsuspecting pit. Within days the whole bunch of us could have held our own against Rudolf Nureyev. With graceful and elastic bounds to any point of the compass we could spring to safety from anything which bore down or fell upon us.

Came the day I reported for actual work. Rising at 4.30 a.m. like some monk and stuffing my pockets with bread and marge plus a round tin can of water, it was Miner Savile reporting for duty, at 6 a.m. at South Kirby colliery, South Yorkshire.

The screens is a job reserved for the young, the old, and the damned. It beats Hell because it's freezing cold. A surface job at sixty feet above ground and best described by the word despair. Let me explain. The coal comes up from the pit mixed with stone. All the stones must be cast aside. This is the stuff most of those great slag heaps are made of. The coal must then be sorted into large and small lumps, and dust. This is where the word 'screens' come from. Long steel trays with holes in them, they crash back and forth. The noise is deafening. The coal is shunted forward, the smaller bits falling through the holes to railway trucks below, and the big bits sliding off into yet more rail trucks alongside.

The noise, the dark, the dust and the torn fingers created an impression of Hell that I will carry to the grave. Each morning after a freezing eternity a small grey square through an unglazed window would herald the dawn. Between 8 a.m. and 8.20 the structure would grind to a halt and we would consume our bread and dust. Peace for twenty whole minutes! Past memories of my after-school job in my beloved dance hall with its whores and hooligans were like a dream that never existed.

Like Oliver Twist, who summoned up his courage to ask for more, I marched to the manager's office to ask to be put to work below ground. It was to be another of my left-handed lucky breaks. There was indeed a job going below. It was peaceful, quiet and I could have it if I wanted. They forgot to mention the fact that the job carried an unusual hazard that sent successive workers screaming into the pit bottom with raving hallucinations.

Imagine a black tunnel three miles long, five feet high, and ten feet wide. At one end is the brightly lit pit bottom, at the other the bustling, busy coalface. After a mile and a half the tunnel suddenly makes a right-hand bend. At this point the endless steel rope that pulls the little trucks of coal runs over a series of steel pulleys which stops the rope biting into the wall of this sharp corner. Should any of the coal tubs leave the track at this bend the damage would be considerable. Therefore a small, inexpensive youth would sit there for eight hours in the pitch dark, and should any recalcitrant truck jump the rails the small inexpensive youth would

20

please turn himself into an incredibly strong gorilla and lift the bleedin' thing back on the rails. The occupational hazard was a simple attack of fright. An hour in the pitch dark is like a year. After four hours you start to hear things. If, after six hours, you haven't hurtled into the pit bottom with every hair standing to attention you are either completely insensitive, or dead.

After the freezing, banging hell of the screens this new job was a warm dark heaven to me. Attacks of fright in plenty did I have but for three and a half years I, was King of the Corner.

As the Chaldean shepherds on their lonely vigil wondered about the night stars, so, after several weeks of staring into the darkness, did I wonder about the nature of things. About people I knew, or sensed, plenty. But about things I was as empty as the darkness. Smuggling books into my exclusive world provided the answers and also a necessary diversion. So engrossed did I become in my learning that the twinkling lights which heralded my returning mates came as an interruption instead of a relief. After three years of six shifts a week living like a walled-up Tibetan monk I was fully conversant with the wonders of astronomy, physics, maths, ancient and modern religions and a variety of languages. 'One off' subjects like politics, economics and world history I treated as light entertainment. This was learning at its most happy. If the mine managers were staggered to find a lad who so took to a terrifying task, I wanted no more than to be left alone.

Instinctively regarded as strange by my mates, there came a day when they drew apart from me and I started to draw apart from the normal world. It all started as a joke on my part.

One can never be late going down the pit, for after a certain time the pit cage is altered to take coal tubs and not men. Because of a transport snag I arrived at the pit top nearly too late to drop, and dressed in my best suit, plus clean white shirt and suede shoes. With no time to change I presented myself to the startled pit bottom bosses as a reincarnation of Beau Brummell. With no explanation forthcoming from me they took in my sartorial magnificence with true Yorkshire silence and off I walked, with my lamp, into the darkness.

Not wanting to damage my only suit and with the normal pit temperature in the 80s, I disrobed once on the job and wrapped all my clothes in newspaper. Sitting around naked for eight hours was no problem. For a laugh I saved some water from my bottle and, cleaning off my hands and face, carefully donned my clothes at the end of the shift. Walking cautiously so as not to disturb the demon dust I reappeared at the pit bottom as immaculate as I had departed. The effect was electric. In the history of coalmining no one had spent eight hours underground and emerged clean. Not a smudge on the collar or cuffs. Witchcraft it may not be but unnatural it certainly was, and I was branded from that moment.

A break in my molelike life came one day with the breathtaking announcement that the buses and trains were on strike twenty-five miles away in Leeds and there was an appeal for volunteer drivers and conductors. In those days such strikes were good-humoured affairs and no one was bothered over a crowd of pit lads all giving false ages in order to drive such tempting juggernauts. Had I been as businesslike then as I am now, a conductor would have been my choice. Several of the lads worked only one day then disappeared—bag, takings and all.

A tram-driver I wanted to be and at 8 a.m. the next morning a dozen of us piled aboard an empty tram and took off for a straight piece of track with preferably not too many pedestrians about. Driven by an inspector who was going to explain the glorious intricacies we were like a bunch of paroled lifers.

The now almost extinct tram was a thing of joy to drive. Like a friendly elephant it would lumber along. Other road-users understood it. On corners it needed a thirty foot arc of clear space, and it got it, for no one would argue with an actual moving friendly neighbourhood tram. If only because it weighed twenty tons.

After half a day's stopping and starting we all finished up back in the tram depot praying that the strike would last long enough for us to realize this incredible windfall. A pimply stripling weighing some seven stone and sporting a pair of spectacles with those lenses like bottle bottoms approached and asked us where tram 46 was. A somewhat strange request as we were sitting on its step. 'Ah, then it's mine,' spake the fearless charioteer. Offering me his temporary licence to view, the boy climbed aboard and positioned himself at the controls. The tram lurched from its resting place. Had one been able to film the following sequence it could have won an Oscar.

Like Boadicea's chariot, scattering all who would bar its path, no. 46 was doing 20 m.p.h. as it burst from the gloom of the tram sheds into a startled Leeds city centre. It crippled three motorcars in as many seconds. The distance from the sheds to the main shopping street, Briggate, is maybe 500 yards. That was as far as he got before running full tilt into the tram in front which had, unwisely, stopped to take on passengers. Several were already aboard before they noticed the rogue tram roaring up the slight incline. As sparrows at the onset of the hawk, passengers and pedestrians took off to all four points of the compass. With a clang of J. Arthur Rank proportions no. 46 ploughed into its luckless stablemate. As with billiard balls, the aggressor stops, but that which is smote moves on. No. 46 was stopped not by its driver who, eye-witnesses have it, left the machine some fifty yards before the impact, but by the simple expedient of having the whole of its front droop onto the floor like the nose of *Concorde*. The other tram, devoid of human life and looking like the *Marie Celeste* on wheels, rolled across the lights at red.

Pursuing their fleeing charge, having wisely abandoned ship, the volunteer conductor and driver legged it down Briggate to the cheers of the onlookers. Order was restored, no. 46 was dragged in backwards, and I was given a chit that said I was the legal driver of tram 39.

It was love at first sight. We emerged daintily from the shed into the sunlight at the regulation five m.p.h. My conductor was a local layabout with a fine sense of occasion. For this occasion he had donned full Royal Navy uniform and, by large tips and short changing the punters, made a fortune in about nine hours.

Seating regulations were not for us and if 150 people wanted to climb aboard a tram designed for 70 who were we to argue. It gave the city a decided atmosphere, with travellers much preferring to hang on, or off, versus walking two or three miles home.

Thereby arose my first disaster.

The weight difference between the empty tram we had trained on and one full of souls was just over double. Ergo, it takes longer to stop. This never occurred to me, and when I spied the railway cart in the distance, pulled by one of those noble shire horses, in theory a gentle application of the handbrake would allow the fine beast of burden plenty of time to get out of the way.

It didn't work out like that.

The wagon was loaded with garden and field produce, in boxes. We caught it a smart crack up the arse and several things happened at the same time. The potatoes and carrots rose out of the boxes like Lazarus from the dead. The driver rose also into the air in a perfect sitting position, at the same time letting go a cry of fear. The magnificent shire horse didn't leave the ground at all, but having had a good belt up the backside from the cart and unable to get a grip on the road with its metal shoes executed a carthorse-on-ice sequence which left its head and shoulders in the doorway of a tobacconist's shop. Piercing screams from within told all that she who was inside was no lover of horses. All this was dwarfed by the cheer which came from our passengers.

Some yards farther along the cheers changed to loud cries of correction as I shot up the wrong road. It was necessary to change the points, at a junction, with a short metal bar, but not having recovered from the horse and cart saga my mind had been elsewhere. A tram takes its power from the bow on its roof which runs along the live overhead wire. If you have to reverse you have to alter the angle of the bow. This is impossible except at certain slack points on the overhead cable. Needless to say I couldn't pull the bow over so we had to navigate the junction with the bow the wrong way.

All went well until we hit the collection of high-voltage wires which make up the overhead junction, when there was a spitting sound from above our heads. Large balls of incandescent material fell all around us. Loud cries of fear came from all aboard. Other trams up and down the same line suddenly went all anaemic and slowed abruptly. Two cars shunted into the back of one, and a lively altercation ensued. This instantly heated discussion was cut somewhat short by my tram clearing the junction and restoring full power down the line, which left two motorists looking at an empty spot where before was a large tram. That particular driver had left his power on full and on resumption of supply had taken off like a dog out of no. 1 box.

This was to be our first, and only, day.

On Kirkstall Road one of my pit colleagues, also misjudging his weight-to-stopping ratio, had serenely borne down upon a coal lorry which was waiting in the middle of the traffic lights to do a right turn. Alarmed by the sight of the tram-driver leaving his clanking charge, together with the more observant of his passengers, the coal-lorry driver (feeling that his end was too nigh for comfort) also left the scene at the double. As the bull gathers the unwary matador so the tram picked up the lorry, turned it on its side and deposited seven tons of coal right across Kirkstall Road, bringing the life of that great artery to a halt. But not for long. Coal was rationed in those days. The sturdy people of the area credited the Good Lord for this manna with loud cries of acclaim: not only had they the road free of coal and into their houses, but they had also righted the lorry, and disappeared.

It was too good to last. The cost and carnage of the volunteer scheme made the dispute resolve itself that very day. Off we went, back to the pit, with memories and cash to sustain us for many a day.

After nearly four years in the deep coal of Yorkshire I managed to get a job at a local pit in Leeds, Waterloo colliery. The coal thickness here was only eighteen inches. It was an old pit with no baths and the most elementary of machinery. We coaxed the coal from its bed with original pick and short-handled shovel. Working in an eighteen inch space means lying on your side for eight hours. The early Romans used to adopt such a position when feasting, but all it did for me was give me a strong feeling of insecurity.

A thin coal seam usually means a bad roof and that keeps one in a state of lively anticipation. The only way out was to wriggle, and in times of stress or possible danger I have been known to cover considerable distances like a serpent. Having always been of a nervous disposition gave me the advantage of being quick off the mark.

Standing near the pit bottom one day there happened that which we miners fear. An accident with the cage halfway up the shaft. Ten tons of coal, several large wooden supports and sundry pieces of broken metal fell amongst us with no warning. In physics there is an atomic mystery where a neutron suddenly disappears from its orbit round a proton and reappears at the same instant, in another place. As the assorted bric-a-brac came cascading down the shaft my helmet was all that was left of me in that position. My disappearance was as instantaneous as the arrival of the goods down the hole. As it happens, no one was hurt and it was all very exciting.

Working at this new pit there was no quiet job for me and my now considerable academic advance was slowed. Instead, I learned to enjoy the delights of real manual labour. There were also pit ponies to handle. Animals were never my strong suit and I don't suppose I rated very high in the ponies' top ten so there was always a lack of harmony between man and beast. The fact that the beast in question was at least ten times as strong as me made it undoubtedly the master. Obviously disgruntled at being entombed alive, the hapless animal would actually pinion me against the wall on occasions and was no fool in a battle of wits. On the way back to the pit-bottom stables we had to climb a steep hill known as a drift, with a gradient of 1 in 3 and 1,000 yards long. It behove the sensible traveller to hang on to the ponies' tackle and be pulled up. Likewise it behove the sensible pony to outwit its masters. One always had to walk behind a pit pony because if you walked in front the beast would just stand still and you'd have to go back for it. Nearing the bottom of the hill my animal would limp, or slow, or have a fit of coughing. Suddenly it would tear off and, if I didn't just catch its tow chain, would leave me well behind on the hill. At the top it would turn and watch my lamp trudging up the slope.

After working for a year with the same beast you strike up a sort of understanding. I'm trying to remember its name but I can't. The only thing that sticks in my memory was its unbelievable capacity for farting. In the twenty-minute peace of my food break it would stand there sounding off and I used to wonder idly if it had any lungs at all or if the air it breathed just carried straight through out the back.

After labouring for two years at Waterloo colliery, and actually quite enjoying the life, I read one day that the cross-Channel ferries had started, with much celebration, the postwar trips from Dover to Calais. The war was only just over and there was a great air of excitement about. We Bevin boys were to be demobbed just like the armed forces and I had two years to go. Freedom was too tempting, and mounting my bike, armed with a magical passport and £15 I cycled 300 miles to Dover.

There was a considerable magic in this brave battered port, the English Channel and that mysterious land, low on the horizon, that only weeks before harboured hostile hordes.

My arrival on the recently raped shores of France was a pantomime. Speaking not a word of the language and having truly the first bicycle to cross into France since the war, the red tape was unbelievable. For three hours I stood on the dockside while officials harangued me, the bike and each other. Finally, because it was getting dark they produced that now familiar French way of life 'the papers of permission to have a bicycle of foreign origin in France'. The papers came in the form of an incredible ledger that weighed all of three pounds that I had to tie across my saddlebag with rope!

A further complication was that all I had in my passport was a transit visa. As it was all in French its meaning had escaped me but apparently France was still closed to all foreigners. By now it was a first-class bureaucratic and physical nightmare so in the gathering gloom I hopped on the bike, rode along the platform, down the sloping bit at the end and out into the ruins of Calais. Nobody shouted after me so there I was, free in France.

The damage of total war in a big city is a thing many have seen but most have not. It is quite impossible to describe. To see acres of half smashed buildings on a film is one thing but to be there, in an atmosphere like a horror movie, is like a nightmare in stereo.

I slept that night in the roofless railway station, Calais Ville, and shared this free lodging with possibly 300 homeless people for whom this was their only refuge. After twenty-four hours of walking about (there was too much rubble to ride), the feeling of near total devastation and not being able to talk to a soul quite unbalanced me. To this day I can close my eyes and see and feel the manmade moonscape of destruction that was the Northern French coast. Imagine what a playground. A drunken looking, smashed house with a German tank half into its wide open living room; piles of ammunition, bullets, machine-gun belts and weapons sometimes three feet high. Anything that was really useful or would burn had been looted days or weeks before.

Actually it was not these first impressions that gave me this everlasting feeling of instant desolation. It was four days later when I arrived in that fashionable pre-war weekend playground of the English rich, Le Touquet. As it happens I very nearly didn't arrive in Le Touquet. About twelve miles to the south of Calais on my second day I had stopped at the top of a rise to view the countryside. About 200 yards behind me a small and ancient lorry turned off into a sort of lay-by and suddenly disappeared into dust and debris with an awful bang. It had run right into a mine—they were still buried in plenty.

Le Touquet at its best is a fairytale place. Villas of the wealthy in colours and fancy dotted in clearings in the superb forest backcloth. Grotesque damage made them look like children's toys smashed by some madman. The centre piece of all this was surely the most beautiful hotel ever built at that time, the Picardy. Perfect in proportion like the Taj Mahal, and built in stone of warm colours to blend with the sun's rays and wooded surrounds, it was for those who saw it a breathtaking building with incredible atmosphere. I first saw it in the early evening light and thought it was a mirage. It looked immaculate and untouched, but as I freewheeled towards it and came out of the evening sun into its shadow it suddenly changed like in a Hitchcock movie. Empty sightless windows peered down. The whole of the inside was shattered. No birds flew about it and the feeling of unreal macabre was overwhelming, like some gigantic tombstone.

That was all I needed and I turned and started slowly off for home pondering on the quite insoluble problem of how people can build things up then knock them down.

Back home in Leeds the inconceivable happened. I had to go back down the pit. Still being under call-up restrictions it was illegal to change my job, so 4.30 a.m. found me a most reluctant hewer of the fossil. To cure me of my wanderlust a stern but not unkind pit boss decreed a spell of night shift. These nocturnal labourings were peopled by confirmed, contented night men who spoke seldom, and those who had sinned against the establishment. Alternately I laboured with the collier equivalent of a Trappist monk and wild rebels, one of whom nearly buried his pick in my head because he had forgotten to bring his chewing tobacco down with him.

At this time came a happening of great import. It was just another shift. My task was called 'belt cleaning'. This entertaining duty was of definitely Dantean quality. Let me explain. As the coal-cutting machine chews up the bottom two inches of the eighteen-inch seam it spits out the resultant dust. This settles on the adjacent floor conveyor belt and has to be shovelled off, or the accumulated weight would be too heavy for the belt to start up on the day shift. A human unit of slender stature must therefore lie full length on the belt and, with a short-handled shovel, clean off the tons of crunched coal dust: a job not guaranteed to raise the spirits of the recently returned continental traveller. A mistake that was nearly to cost me my life was simple.

The coal seam with a two-inch gap at its base is now ready for 'shot firing'. Into round holes previously drilled into the coal are fitted small explosive charges. These are detonated and it is advisable that frail humans should gather at a respectful distance. The man who detonates the shot looks down the face to check that no lights, the miner's constant friend, are visible. No one had told me of this hazard and my light happened to be on the wrong side of the belt.

Once again I had elected, albeit innocently, to join the Good Lord's heavenly hordes, but again He gave me the brush-off. Instead I was deafened by a compressive 'whump' and my cry of terror echoed down the face.

Slightly concussed by the close blast and covered in debris plus one large stone which had blown down off the roof, I was pulled clear by the lads. Again a miracle as I was totally unmarked, but my legs moved in a funny sort of way. It is a normal thing for miners to make light of whatever personally befalls them; not through any heroics, it's just the way it is. Assuring all that all was well with me I laid down for the rest of the shift and went to sleep. During the next few days all my aches and pains disappeared except the one in my back. This got steadily worse till I walked about like Pisa's famous landmark. After two weeks it added a sort of Chesterfield spire effect to my leaning act so off I went to hospital.

Medical workers will tell you that the worst sort of patient is one who feels the pain but X-rays can't see it. So I was fitted out with a surgical webbing corset with steel rods in it, which I keep as a souvenir to this day. This jolly garment had the effect of straightening me up like a guardsman but made me unable to lift my feet off the ground more than an inch. Also I kept falling over like a drunk. Two walking sticks were added to my survival kit and hey presto I was released into the free world, after seven event-filled years underground.

I was also given sixteen shillings a week sick money.

Trying to live on less than a pound a week has several advantages. I've forgotten what they are and don't ever want to re-discover them, but yet I was not unhappy. A bed, a radio, super parents who were poor in pocket but rich in understanding: it was all quite peaceful and lovely really. But of course it couldn't stay like that. The majority of humans aren't built to take peace and loveliness for too long. We all seem to want to get on and get somewhere. Though what, and where, the 'somewhere' is is anybody's guess. True to form and anxious to increase my income I pinned up the picture of a Rolls-Royce car on the inside of my wardrobe door. None of our family had ever possessed a motorbike let alone a car but a picture would do for a start.

A friend of mine was winning a few elusive pounds in his spare time by manufacturing ladies' brooches out of plaster of paris. It took thirty minutes of industrial espionage to win his secrets and with the help of several sticks of plasticine and a borrowed brooch depicting a negroid head, hey presto, we were off.

My manufacturing area was the kitchen sink and my first efforts succeeded in blocking the entire plumbing system with the concrete-like substance which is plaster of paris when not flushed away. Undeterred by such hold-ups the brooches were soon coming off my assembly line, and after ten hours of feverish labour I finished up with fifty finished pieces. Selling them proved to be a problem as the only gilt paint around at that time adhered to fingers and clothes like gold dust. The project was not a marked success and I returned to my bed, radio, peace and loveliness to try and work things out.

Using a sort of back-to-front logic I reasoned that if I made a list of all the things and sensations that I liked, it would be a good idea to try and make money and have a good time at the same time. Utopia they call it, but where is it?

Another friend of mine had made up a strange machine from the innards of an extinct radio. This affair, when connected to his wind-up gramophone, produced music on a grand scale. It was to the present hi-fi sets what the Wright brothers' first efforts were to *Concorde*. Hearing of this via the complaining mothers' grapevine I hurried to inspect his important discovery as fast as sticks and corset would allow. A short demonstration was all I needed to realize its potential. I mean, music by Glenn Miller and Harry James in larger than life quantity: it had to be worth something. A swift fifty-fifty deal was concluded. At this point it is worth noting that such a percentage I have never given away since.

A hall was booked for ten shillings from 7 till 10 p.m. Both of our mothers were commissioned to produce refreshments and teas for the expected multitudes. Friends were advised of fantastic entertainment to be had on the evening in question for the payment of one shilling admission.

The night itself is worthy of note. Installing the equipment was fraught with great dangers. It was in several pieces connected by wires. These covered the top of a grand piano, glowed red hot when switched on for longer than five minutes, and charred the top of that noble instrument for the rest of its days. Unwary handling resulted in the operator being immediately electrocuted and, half an hour before opening time, plunged the hall in darkness by blowing the main fuse.

By 9 p.m. we had taken eleven shillings, the machine had melted at several soldered points and died quietly, but not before giving a final electric shock to its inventor causing him to weep openly. All was nearly lost. My mother was called in from the refreshment room to play the grand piano but her music was not our music and anyway the smell of recent burning from its polished lid made her feel off. Our efforts were applauded by all present, all expenses were waived by tacit understanding and my pal and I pocketed five and six each.

Disaster or not, dear reader, there can be no doubt that the world's first disco, as they have come to be called, took place in the top room of the Belle Vue Road branch of the Loyal Order of Ancient Shepherds and they can now have the ten bob I owe them anytime they want.

Nothing daunted I commissioned the manufacture of an electric gramophone of sufficient durability to withstand four hours of constant operation. For among my first paying customers had been a young lady shortly to celebrate her twenty-first and she booked me at the staggering fee of £2 10s. providing I could last the night.

This was to be a night of heady success. It was a room in a café in Otley, in the Yorkshire Dales, and after the tea tables had been cleared dancing would commence. Operating on my own I contrived to connect my new machine the wrong way round. There is in the world of amplifiers a technical definition known as 'open circuit negative feedback'. This is a noble term for a noble sound. It is a shriek of ear-splitting density and one which causes dogs at considerable distance to flee under sideboards and bark with equal gusto. When suddenly unleashed on people of normal hearing, after a good meal, and in a medium-sized room, it can create a lively scene, unrivalled in the field of unexpected noises.

In my case it had the instant effect of causing all the guests but one to rise off the floor a good twelve inches. The one exception was the grandmother of the birthday girl who, at eighty-two, fell off her chair and suffered an immediate swoon. Apart from this one hitch it was, as I said, a night of heady success and such a good time was had by all, including me, that I forgot to get paid.

The girl in question, being honest, remembered and rushed back, putting two pound notes and a ten shilling one in my hand, and dashed out. Looking at this vast sum of money, more than I had ever earned in my life, I realized, most definitely and positively, that I had arrived at the threshold of a fortune! But cash in considerable quantities, like the mystic mirage, is there for all to see but deuced difficult to actually get your hands on.

To say the British public were somewhat slow in taking advantage of my new dimension of enjoyment, the recorded music dance, would be an understatement. Many a sharp practice had to be employed in order not to lose money. On one occasion I took a disused barn. One dozen people turned up. The taxi fare home came to more than the take as the dance wouldn't finish till after the last bus had gone. But, as always, deliverance was just round the corner. At half time, spurning the barn-owner's tea and buns, the entire audience trooped off to the fish shop. On their return, lo, all was locked up and in darkness. Father Jim and his infernal machine were safely on the last bus with a profit of nearly one pound. Of such things is a super life made.

My back was getting better. The steel corset was only needed for the odd hour and my sticks had been relegated to the hallstand. As a therapy and to compensate for my years of entombment I discovered farming camps. This most excellent national effort, the Lend a Hand on the Land scheme, was really fantastic. From all parts of the country, and indeed the world, young people worked on farms for 1s. 6d. an hour. Living together in disused prisoner-of-war camps life was totally full of all that was good. I would spend three months of the year stripped to the waist, labouring like I was back down the pit, but how wonderful not to bump your head or skin your knees. The other nine months I was a big local impresario. Penniless, but with a dress suit no less.

Unfortunately time passed too quickly too pleasantly, and I was getting nowhere. One discovery I had made during my pursuit of the tuber and grain was, of all things, a natural and almost disastrous power of hypnotism. After a day in

35

the fields, most of the campers would topple on their beds as the felled tree. The rest of us would gather round a real fire in the common room after lights-out and talk. Somehow the conversation turned to hypnotism and as a joke I professed to possess the powers. To demonstrate, and choosing a girl who was already fast asleep in her easy chair, I stood behind her. Miracle of miracles, with eyes fast closed she answered all my stage-whispered questions. Passing myself off as first her mother, then father, and finally boyfriend we had a lively patter going that reduced the firelight audience to tears. I was convinced she was awake and just playing along with me. Taking again the part of her mother and asking her what on earth she was doing in bed with all her clothes on, sweet horror, did she not stand up and start to undress.

I was reduced to a jelly with fright. A sign of the unpermissive times was that the room emptied in a second. Telling her to stop, and in the nick of time as it had been a warm evening, she was handed to her girlfriend with instructions to put her to bed. The next morning, expecting to be denounced and dismissed, I was shattered with relief when she stood next to me in the breakfast queue and gave not the slightest sign of recognition.

Years later in the Isle of Man I met Josef Karma, one of the great hypnotists. Telling him the story, he was not surprised at all and suggested I should study under him for a while so that my natural gift, which he subsequently confirmed, would enable me to do good, and not finish up in the nick!

CHAPTER THREE

For those of us strange band of humans who are not content with a normal way of working life it behoves us to take constant stock of how we're going on. The dance hall business suited me but as it didn't make me rich it was obviously my fault. I knew that my record sessions were a good idea and worked out that the day would come. Now obviously I had to be ready for that day and there was much I must learn. One of the faults of being a live wire is that you think you don't have to learn anything. Without the discipline and grind of big business routine you are a dead duck. Example. I was once giving a lecture in a university and one of the students, fired by my straight talking, came across a great opportunity which he took. In no time at all he had £20,000 in the bank and in no time at all someone took it off him. His good idea was a one-off and he is now working for a living and much wiser—and still looking for his next opportunity at which time he will be much more businesslike.

So, where was I to find my necessary grinding and shaping? As usual I landed right side up and took an offered job as an assistant manager, at £8 10s. a week, in the very dance hall I had worked in during the war, whilst at school. How super it was to be back and how right it felt. The daily routine nearly broke my spirit. Gone was the wind whispering through the grass. No more the satisfaction of seeing a whole field of wheat well stooked. Instead it was drunken bums arguing to come in, lost coats in the cloakroom, and the ever-present possibility of getting your head kicked in.

Still broke and choosing not to live at home, for the soft life is not good for the would-be self-made man, where to live, for nothing, was a problem. For some weeks I slept on the floor of my changing room and was very comfortable. One day I learned of a disused ex-lifeboat turned into a motor launch. This was moored in a most noxious and inaccessible tie-up on the canal that ran through the centre of Leeds. If I could keep it afloat by regular pumping and pay the 3s. 6d. weekly mooring fee it was mine until it sank.

For a year it was my freezing home and for a year no two nights were the same. It was tied up about fifty feet from a thunderous weir. To reach my constantly tossing haven was like a suicidal aqua Grand National. First one had to cross a builder's yard strewn with leg-breaking obstacles. Then a painter's plank spanned an inky void on to a derelict barge. This was in an advanced stage of decay and the unwary step would drop you like Sweeney Todd's chair into the bowels of the boat where lived rats and noisome suchlike. After the barge it was a short jump across to my lodgings. The lodgings had a nasty habit of shying away and turning a four-inch jump into a six-foot Beechers. Once gained, the boat turned into a paradise.

The waterway was half canal and half river. Like the sea it was ever changing and dangerous. One morning, awakened by cries of warning from the builders on the bank, I rushed up top in time to see the rivers in full, angry spate and a large tree or telegraph pole bearing down upon the raging waters. Seizing a boathook I rushed to the side to fend off that which threatened my abode, ignoring the shouted advice to abandon ship. The log or pole rushed by like a submarine, shot over the weir at a great rate of knots and impaled a steel coal barge which promptly sank amid loud cries from the colliers.

On another occasion I awoke feeling a distinct list on the bunk. All was black out of the windows therefore all was not well as it should have been daylight. Up on deck a strange sight awaited me for I was in another world. Me and the boat were in a muddy hole some thirty feet deep and there was no water. The river and canal had completely disappeared. The truth of the matter was that at a certain time of the year, and on a Sunday, the water was diverted so that the weir could be cleared of debris. Not knowing of this and at a loss to understand this incredible drought I reasoned that some cataclysm had overtaken the area. To climb out of that mud-coated amphitheatre took me over an hour and was the sort of stuff that Charlie Chaplin films were made of. Such lodgings are the stuff of magic.

Two hundred miles away in the Mecca head office in London, my qualifications, or rather peculiarities, had not gone entirely unnoticed. Their dance hall in Ilford was not too healthy and a new manager was needed. I was summoned at once to fill this powerful post. Here was success after only a short time as dogsbody assistant manager.

I had never even slept overnight in London before so every experience in that great fishing port was new. Likewise, Ilford had never adopted a strange provincial stripling before, so a lively scene of regional adjustment was necessary.

Many words have been written and spoken about the differences between the denizens of the north and south. The simple answer is that only the values of things differ, not really the people. For instance, traffic. When faced with London traffic circumnavigating Hyde Park Corner the northerner imagines he is in the middle of the Charge of the Light Brigade and, fearing for his life, has been known to be trapped in the inside lane and go round and round and even come to a full stop. London traffic then goes round and round him throwing out the obligatory curse. All of which is taken personally by the dour northerner and he returns home with tales of the mad motoring metropolis and leaves his car at Watford next time.

For the reverse, take snow. A light covering of snow over the capital causes excited discussion on trains and the snow is gazed upon with distrust. Russian-style hats appear in the street and the loyal Londoner strides manfully about in scarf and gloves. In the north a force ten gale in winter is dismissed as a bit windy.

In the south, reputation also plays a big part. One of our local lads was described to me in terms that would have got him a place in any Mafia family. In the two years I enjoyed the area's hospitality he never struck a blow or pulled a job but still enjoyed his Joe Bananas reputation to the day I left.

Apart from the wonderful time I had with my new East End friends, my sojourn in the south was historic for one stupendous happening. My reluctant invention and pet, the public performance of records, transformed the dance hall, the capital, eventually the entire country, and finally, the whole world.

At a historic meeting between myself and the top Mecca directors it was decided that, on payment of the vast sum of one shilling admission, the guys and gals of the Ilford watershed could have a great night out with, at long last, me and my machine. It wasn't supposed to be quite like that because it was unthinkable that a Mecca manager should don clothes other than evening dress let alone mount the stage for anything longer than one announcement.

In fact, a few days later I walked in the dance hall and found the record equipment being installed up in the lighting control room. Enough of such reticence. The old order of the cinema projectionist putting on a record in the interval was to be destroyed. The disc jockey was about to make his first stage appearance in mighty London Town.

To make sure that my sparsely populated Yorkshire nights were not repeated I had invited the entire audience in for free the first night. It was a Tuesday night and the previous week's business had netted twenty-four souls. Southerners have a keen nose for a happening and before the doors opened a large crowd was milling without. The notice admitting all free was hastily altered by hand, mine, to read 'Until 8.30 p.m.' 500 beautiful, miraculous people poured in by 8.30. On a stage littered with those brittle 78 r.p.m. records I dispensed music at a volume never before heard. For four hours I socked it to 'em and was quite light-headed with the success of it all. From 8.30 onwards slightly over 500 patrons not only willingly parted with a shilling each but actually jostled to get in. Over 1,000 admissions compared with the previous week's twenty-four!

And that was only the first night. After four weeks I was playing to 2,000 paying customers. The dancing world had been stunned and it was 'look out here we come' for Jimmy Savile.

Ideas which are considered wild and foolish when one is penniless suddenly become genius and brilliant in the eyes of the world as soon as one starts to make money. Therefore, an idea which would surely have got me the sack before was hailed now as a master stroke.

My hall had to run a heat of a national beauty contest called the Queen of Light. Never liking to do anything in the normal way I pondered on how to make it different. For some few nights I had been intrigued by a happening in the road just outside the front door of the ballroom.

Round about 8.30 p.m. every night along would come six solemn gents wheeling a large cart. Showing a great dexterity of footwork equal to my best dancers, they would set up a base camp complete with red lights slap in the middle of this busy main road. This alone was worth watching as the traffic was mad and furious at all times. They never got knocked down but several roadwork-type red lights shone their last after being flattened by some road hog. The language and sprightly jumpings out of the way were better some nights than others but the end product was always the same. A large manhole in the centre of the road was uplifted and all six gents descended into the depths and remained incommunicado for several hours. It was this disappearing act which intrigued me and when I went to look down the hole there issued not the faintest sound but a most incredible pong. Without going into details suffice to say that these men worked the sewers and became my friends.

Back to the beauty contest, and I had altered the papers to cover it as it would be unlike any other. Up turned the press and about twenty-five beautiful competitors.

Working the opposite way round I brought all the girls on stage first in a long, lovely line. In full toastmaster emotion I then announced the judges. At this juncture the double doors at the opposite end of the hall swung open and, in line abreast, complete with rubber thigh boots and overalls, advanced my six sewermen friends—of course, the judges.

In the unlikely event of such a competition being held in Moscow, no more thunderous applause could have been given to the workers than on that night. The girls in their swimsuits collapsed with laughter, the crowd cheered and cheered, the judges, overcome, waved like the royals they were. It was a splendid scene. The six lads took their time on the verdict and there were more thunderous cheers as they drew out baccy tins and made themselves roll-up cigs.

A worthy winner was chosen and crowned, but all was not yet finished. Having explained to the patrons the true labours of my friends the judges, the entire ballroom emptied, girls and all, and we stood and cheered as the lads did the grand finale of disappearing down the manhole. A great night with great publicity and it was difficult for head office to argue with success.

With things going great guns in Ilford I was promptly transferred to another hall that was doing duff business, the Plaza, Manchester. The stories of my three years in that truly wonderful city would make a book on their own. Two good strokes of commercial luck fell my way. One was an incredibly efficient secretary. Without one of these any businessman is doomed. The other was my local boss, dead now, God rest his soul, called Jack Binks. 'J.B.' as we called him

42

owned the centre of Manchester above the legal line so I rapidly took control of the town below it.

When one is saddled with a bad business hall, reputation is not enough. You have to deliver the goods at the box office. The local male wolves were startled to see a large poster outside my front door announcing 'Saturday Night is Crumpet Night'. In those non-permissive days this was equal to showing a nude photo of Marilyn Monroe ten feet high. For three days this excited the populace no end and on the fourth J.B. came back from an out of town trip. In a phone call charged with outrage I was ordered to take it down forthwith. Having foreseen this instruction and good obedient lad that I was, down it came. But only to reveal another poster beneath announcing 'Saturday for KIFE'. Kife by the way is the nautical and armed forces' equivalent for Crumpet.

The offending Crumpet poster was ceremonially torn up in the boss's office. Subsequent stories reaching him about 'that' poster he presumed to be about the recently destroyed one. When he realized I had worked a flanker I was definitely due for the chop. Just in the nick of time Saturday night turned up and instead of the usual handful of patrons, we were turning them away. And like I said before, it's very difficult to argue with success. As I said to the boss, 'It's all in the mind; to the pure, all things are pure.'

A new session was invented in Manchester. Lunchtime dancing. At threepence a head, from midday till 2 p.m. this was to become a way of life for many. Once again my record playing act on stage within four days packed the hall to capacity. Its official capacity was 450 but during the two hours we could turn over 2,000 souls. So popular was it after a week that I promptly doubled the admission to sixpence!

Life was now too good to be true. My memory, ever photographic, remembered my early, empty barns and rooms in cafés and I determined not to get too clever too quick. There was a simple formula for success. Give people a good time but stand no nonsense from anyone. Good-fun publicity is the key to open the minds of the people to your presence among them.

In those days a flash car was always good publicity. With no cash for flash, as it were, it was back to my, by now, tried and proven think tank. Somehow I managed to scrape up the deposit for an old Bentley saloon. Not letting this be seen around the town, it was run into another garage. From a scrap shop was purchased a modern Rolls Royce radiator. After lots of hammering, welding and spraying of paint there emerged into a startled Manchester what appeared to be a new black and cream Rolls Royce. Belonging to me, no less! Great was the appreciation of my customers, for teenagers like to see their leaders do well.

On close examination the car provided a lively discord. Things like a Rolls radiator but Bentley wheeldiscs caused much conjecture, but only among the wealthy purists. One of the younger reporters on the powerful *Manchester Evening News* came to marvel at the sleek beast and suggested a picture of me alongside it, on my bike. We shot the picture on what's called a slow news day so, miracle of miracles, it finished up right across the front page. When asked the price of a new Rolls I had mentioned the true figure of £7,500. This was not a lie because the unfortunate reporter had not asked the price of my particular hybrid. Letters poured into the newspaper pointing out finer points of doubt. The car was promptly hidden away and I was left juggling with my boss who wanted to know where the hell I'd got £7,500 and the motoring correspondent of the paper asking for a look-see. After four days they were all too busy to bother and the shining trouble-causer reappeared outside my dance hall and gathered admiring crowds of passers-by.

Business boomed and the Plaza became a way of life for well behaved pleasure seekers. Three days a week we ran private dances and we rapidly filled all vacant dates. Great fun, these private functions with churches, charities and firms.

My payments on the car left no money for cigars, and they were a flash necessity, so my nightwatchman had every night the immediate task of going round the ashtrays and selecting the larger dog ends. These shortened, but when lit impressive, impedimenta confirmed that I was loaded. Who else but a loaded lad could chainsmoke cigars and have a new Rolls outside the door?

Our big prestige night came with the booking of an Italian dance. No less a personage than the Ambassador was coming from London. In company with our own Lord Mayor they arrived just as I was organizing a spot dance so they were seated in my office. Rushing to greet them I suddenly realized that having never met either of them, I wouldn't know which one was the Ambassador. What didn't help was that they were both wearing full medal and sash honours. Quick as a flash I bowed low at the two magnificent men and said 'Good evening Excellency.' Straightening up from my jacknife position, the one with his hand stuck out to shake was the Ambassador.

With a bit of quick thinking and a lot of luck, you don't need brains.

With the clergy I formed a sort of manager's office club. At a church dance, the bottle of sherry and glasses would always be set out on my desk and all the priests would come in first and have a quick snifter. Great chaps priests, full of laughter and practical jokes. There was one who was madly good-looking and the ladies adored him. We all used to pull his leg about this and he would give as good as he got. One day I received an anonymous love letter headed 'My Darling'. It went on to arrange a tryst in the dance hall and told me to look out for her long red hair. As the letter could have been for anyone, the other villain priests put it on the sherry tray in an envelope marked for the good-looking one.

45

Enter the film star Father and, selecting his glass of cheer, sees the letter and, suspecting nothing, takes it to read. After the first two lines, it disappears into his pocket quicker than a wedding tip. Off he goes into my washroom and we all die with suppressed laughter. An ashen priest reappears and pours himself a large drink. The others, realizing that the fish is firmly on the hook, urge him to go into the dance and mix with the faithful. Fearful that one of the faithful might have long red hair and be obviously far more lustful than filled with faith, our chum cleric insisted he needed another, and another, until he was finally overcome by the brew. So his pals shipped him out of the side door and back to his presbytery. They all voted it the best dance ever. Too late did the poor priest realize he'd been tricked, but he keeps the letter to this day as a great souvenir.

To run a dance hall is better than running a harem because all your wives go off home to reappear, fresh and lovely, the next night. There are two reasons why I could not tell the story of all the girls I have known. One is because I respect and would you believe love them for their incredible days, and nights. The other is that, were I to tell all, no one would believe it, plus I'd have to take up residence in some inaccessible Himalayan village. Rarely if ever do I go to parties as I always seem to finish up in some trouble not of my seeking. Being a personality, even then, makes the world a far different place than if you are normal. At one party I narrowly escaped being knifed, with a breadknife as it happens, by a slightly intoxicated young lady who disapproved of a girl she didn't like sitting on my knee.

Another near disaster party was an incredible event. It was held in a house in Sale, Cheshire. The owner had taken a hurt that I always knocked his invitation back, so, much against my will, I went to a gathering of not more, he assured me, than a dozen people. As I drove there a foolproof plan formulated in my mind. The first girl I found who was on her own would be mine for all to see. I invariably went every-where alone, and still do, and a single supposedly wealthy man causes much trouble among semi-intoxicated wives, fiancées and their men-folk. So it was into the house, shake all round, and settle down to find a loner girl. By far the most attractive girl in the room was sitting on the floor playing records. There was no time for finesse as all the ladies present had perked up at the prospect of a ride off in a Rolls and a lovely row when they got home. And me with my head cracked open later.

'Who did you come with?' says I.

'No one,' says she.

For the next one hour there was no doubt in anyone's mind that she was my girl. Dancing closer than a stamp to a letter, with many a caress and a wink to the other guys in the room, it was all turning into a rather super evening and all this display of loving feeling was getting me at it. So it was time for the hawk to carry the captive dove off to its nest. Boy, was I in for a surprise.

'Who did you come with?' says I knowingly.

'Came on my own,' says she with her fingers locked in my hair.

'So who are you going home with?' says I with confident expectation.

'My husband,' was the incredible reply.

My heart did a quick somersault.

'But you said you came on your own,' says I with a sudden body temperature of minus ten.

'I did,' she purred. 'He was already here.'

There come times in the life of man when he wishes he really wasn't where he actually was. I claim to be a contender for the world championship for that feeling.

'So where is he?' says the voice of my long-dead grand-father; actually it was mine but I didn't recognize it.

'Sitting in a chair behind you.'

47

A Christian in the Colosseum never felt the lions breath down the back of his neck so real.

Not to bore you with details of personal terror, suffice to say that my original plan had turned into the original sin. Exit stage left was a necessity. Sauntering off to the loo like the Godfather it was a case of wedging the door with paper to save the next client having to break in. The window was easy and only six feet from the ground. Out of it and into the car and away.

The next day my host telephoned. 'It's no wonder you never go to parties. You are a diabolical bastard to carry on with that poor guy's wife like that.' There was no point in my explaining, so yet another piece of legend was hung on to my life tree.

Round about this time, with the financial situation reasonably rosy and success coming as an expectation rather than a surprise, I was able to share some of the good times with relatives and friends. The Duchess would come over to Manchester and we would have sumptuous lunches which made her very proud. I wasn't able to give her anything like the pocket money she deserved, or needed, for cash was not all that plentiful, but facilities were. It is very pleasant to entertain one's parent in luxury surroundings and makes life very sweet.

At one of these lunches she mentioned in conversation an old retired uncle of mine who envied, in the nicest possible way, her trips to me. Many were the school holidays I had spent at his South Shields home so a telegram was dispatched immediately. 'Come and spend a week with me in Manchester.' Uncle Sid was his name, well over seventy was his age, and he was to prove one of the great characters of that great city.

Uncle Sid had spent his life on the north-east coast as an insurance agent, and, miraculously, had never seen a skyscraper building. As he was only five feet tall they looked even higher to him.

At the time I was driving a flash white drophead Buick and it was leaning against this that I waited for his arrival at the station. Complete with dark glasses I looked the picture of this year's playboy. Needless to say he didn't recognize me and, when he did, was speechless with the picture of such opulence belonging to a relative. The luxury of my dance hall and office stunned him even further.

Putting a fifty box of cigs and a bottle of whisky on the desk I told him, 'Let me know when you've finished 'em, there's plenty more.'

We had a week that beggars description.

Uncle Sid stories I could tell you for hours. How he made himself a king on the social scene will do for a start.

In those days late-night drinking clubs were illegal but Manchester had several, all of magnificent, earthy character, and I doubt if such clubs will ever be seen again. One of these was called the Motor Club. Entrance was effected by methods seen only in early gangster movies. Delivering a sharp rap on a door in a dark side street, the thirsty client was ushered into a genuine warehouse. Modestly lit by un-shaded bulbs the route then lay past piles of boxes to an open cage-type lift. This ancient transport lurched upwards and out one stepped amidst more industrial impedimenta. Another knock on another door and voilà! Shangri La! An elegant and warm room filled with folk and bonhomie awaited the thirsty traveller. Actually there was a front door to this room but as it was in Bootle Street, opposite the central police station, it was not much used. I had phoned the owner, explained my temporary guest, and asked that all present should address him as Uncle Sid so he would really feel at home.

The doors, the dark warehouse, the lift and finally the elegant club rendered my magnificent, immaculate and tiny

Uncle Sid once more speechless. Sat on a tall stool by the bar he consumed his whisky and shook hands with one and all, bewildered by the fact that they all addressed him by name like old friends. What really socked Uncle Sid for six was that he was next to a fruit machine. Of these he had seen plenty at his seaside home but was staggered to see that this one consumed half crowns, not pennies. After watching one client put six quid in and get nowt out, that was the end. At 5 a.m. I carried him out and put him to bed.

The next day, in my office, another dear and personal friend of mine, Louis Harper, called. He was Louis the Lion, Chief Superintendent of Police for Manchester A Division, copper par excellence, terror of tearaways, and a real legendary character. He was duly introduced to Uncle Sid and solemnly accepted some of his whisky. 'How do you like Manchester then?' asked the king of coppers.

Uncle's mistake was presuming that all friends of mine were, therefore, friends of each other.

'Wonderful,' says Uncle. 'That club last night was fantastic. Just fancy drinking till 5 a.m.'

'Oh,' says Louis. 'Tell me about it, Uncle.'

A vivid description of illegal night life was rounded off with a graphic description of the machine that gobbled up half crowns.

'See,' says Uncle Sid, 'the owner gave me his card.'

Louis sipped his whisky and turned the card over. Taking his pen out he put his autograph on the back. Uncle Sid had, in his innocence, totally destroyed an illegal undertaking, but it spoke volumes for Louis's methods as he said, 'There, Uncle Sid, that's a museum piece now. Tell the owner I'm glad you had a good time.'

The final scene was to play. Later that night Uncle and I were back at the club. Last night he had been a novelty, tonight he was history. Or so they thought. Out of friendship to me the owner moved across the floor to sit by us at the bar.

'How's things today Uncle Sid?' says he with his mind on other things.

'Wonderful,' says Uncle. 'I had a good drink today with your friend Louis Harper.'

The club-owner, Ronnie, seemed to have some trouble with his swallowing mechanism.

'Yes,' says Uncle Sid, turning the screw, 'he said he'd never been here and was very interested in your half crown fruit machines.'

Ronnie turned pale and closed his eyes.

'Look,' said Uncle Sid, 'he even signed the back of your card.'

'Aaarrrhhh,' says Ronnie as if seized by some internal spasm.

At this point it was necessary for me to stop the rot. I explained to Ronnie it might be a good idea to get rid of the machines as Louis didn't like them, but I doubted if he would be raided as Uncle Sid had spoken so highly of the premises.

This caused two reactions. Ronnie first broke into an actual sweat of relief at the saving of his £1,000 a week income, and, as Uncle Sid was the saviour, Ronnie called the room to order, told the story, put Uncle Sid on free booze for life and declared that Uncle be given the freedom of Manchester. Or at least the Manchester underworld.

And so he reigned. The five foot, innocent, King of the Night Life. Fêted and treated wherever I chose to take him.

Three memorable visits did Uncle Sid make from South Shields to Manchester.

Oh, something I didn't tell you, from before I sent the telegram, which was *why* I sent the telegram. Uncle Sid was dying of cancer. Of course he didn't know, and when I got the phone call that told me he had been taken to hospital for the grand finale, I climbed into my big car and drove the 150 miles to his side. As I walked in the ward his bright eyes followed me all the way down. There was nothing to say. He knew. Tears twinkled in his eyes like diamonds and I took his hand.

A picture tells more than a thousand words but a touch means more than a thousand pictures. I left him, with a pain in me as real as a wound, and drove back to Manchester. The town never felt so empty.

Life goes on, as we all know, but it's never quite the same when a piece of your heart has gone for ever. How many pieces does a human heart hold? How much of it can we lose before we lose it all, and ourselves?

CHAPTER FOUR

After three and a half glorious years in that great Lancashire city and having won two awards for top successful dance hall business it was time to move.

The final act in my dance hall career was to be played. By incredible concidence the very hall where I first started, playing the drums in the girls' band whilst at school, the Mecca in Leeds, was in dead trouble. Business was non-existent and it was down and out. A clear case for the touch of the, by now, master.

There have been successes in the dance hall business but never the spectacular, literally overnight success of my arrival back in my home town. It is written for ever, in the minutes of the parent company, by the then Managing Director, Walter J. Pickard. It reads like a citation and he had it put that way on purpose.

With my usual incredible luck, the day I took up the Leeds job coincided with the holidays of several key directors at head office. The opportunity was too good to miss. Basic policy changes which would have taken some days, and meetings, to O.K. were carried out in an instant. Not only in an instant, but on a whim. Having a packed house for my first pop record night, I suddenly stopped the music. 'Is it a good night then?' I asked. 'Yes,' answered a thousand voices. 'Same deal then tomorrow night, O.K.?' And so they all turned up on the morrow. And the next and the next. It was as simple as that. Everyone wanted to see this impossible disc jockey who was also the general manager, who would suddenly cut the sound and say 'How's about I should let you all in for nothing tomorrow?' By the time the directors returned not only was the policy unrecognizable, the cash

53

flow was unbelievable and I had a large 'House Full' sign which went up every night at 9.30. Four nights of the week it wasn't really full but the people who were turned away didn't know that so the legend grew and that's really where a lot of the success came from.

A good thing should be easy to recognize and it was quite by chance I stumbled on what was to be my crowning glory, in more ways than one. Some juniors from a ladies' hair salon were dance regulars and asked me if I'd like a free hair do. Until then the idea of entering a ladies' salon had never occurred to me, but having a weakness for girls in that employ, along I went. It was student practice night so I suggested they should turn me into a raving blond. A cold goo was slapped onto my unsuspecting bonce and I was left to cook. After a while it felt that I was being slowly trepanned without anaesthetic. With eyes watering freely and a voice like the snake's in *Jungle Book*, I suggested that all might not be well with their concoction.

All was not well and several layers of skin had been consumed by their fiery potion. The students, in a great tizzy, promptly phoned their respected lady boss and she came post haste through the night. The voracious bleach was removed by washing and a medical disinfectant was applied. This transaction took me to a pain level equal to gala night at the Spanish Inquisition.

Dwelling on the female proverb 'pride is painful' I went back to the dance hall—and brought the place to a screaming standstill. Marilyn Monroe never had it so good. Cries of delight, derision and disbelief filled the night. Only those who have dramatically and suddenly changed their hairstyle will know the startling effect it has on their friends. As I had over 1,000 friends in the hall at the time it created a stupendous reaction.

My animal logic reasoned that reaction of this magnitude could be cash in the bank. Over the next few weeks a glittering technicolour display shone from my multi-coloured head. Now the 'House Full' sign really meant what it said.

By now the hair salon, Muriel Smith's, and I had embarked on the road of no return. Joe, the owner, had taken charge of my body above the eyebrows and two weeks was the longest breathing space my scalp was allowed before the next iridescent onslaught. After a few months we had used up all the colours on the chart and were stumped, but not for long. 'How about a nice tartan?' says I to Joe. Game for anything, he worked out a plan of attack. At a secret session with only one assistant, and a six hour operation, the style to end all styles walked out of the shop.

Dress Stewart Tartan.

Pictures of this creation actually went right round the world.

It requires considerable strength to walk around sporting such tonsorial trauma. It also causes damage to those who come upon you unexpectedly. The nearest my hair got to manslaughter was on a train from Leeds to London. Really I should have worn a cap when mixing with the public but I would actually forget what I was sporting. Breezing into the dining car, my tartan hair so startled one of the customers that his pre-dinner drink went down the wrong 'ole. It got quite serious, with the unfortunate chap doing an aurora borealis of the features and frightening sounds from deep within. By this time we had him stretched out on his face and as many good samaritans as could get near were practising long forgotten respiration aids.

To live a normal life again suddenly seemed very desirable so we had to coax my tartan locks back to an innocent blond. On went the fiery bleaches but the Scottish influence was not that easy to dismiss. I was left with a patchwork of dots, flecks and odd stripes. Joe was perturbed for the rightful good name of his salon. The world's hair press was waiting for the next creation. It wasn't long in coming. A light grey rinse, a bit of fluffing up and, hey presto, Harris Tweed!

Locally I was now considered a cross between Medusa and Carmen Miranda. Praise was showered on Joe and me but no one realized we were stumped for what to do next.

To go back dark would be an anticlimax but to let it grow out would take six months. Cheerful as ever we locked the doors and set to once more. A platinum rinse was heated over a flame and the resultant molten mixture ladled onto the battleground of my head. The texture of my scalp was by now equal to a camel's backside and completely impervious to assault.

The chemical reaction of this latest concoction caused my locks to take on a chromium plated effect. The well faded cross stripes gave a strange opaque effect, so, lo, Mother of Pearl!

Leaving this for a month, the next routine took us back to square one, a nice simple blond. Such a relief it was to come down from super-abnormal to plain old abnormal.

It was in Leeds I won the Gold Cup award for dance hall business. As Mecca was the world's largest company in this field it automatically made me the world's top manager. My strange ways of going on created an unusual company situation. As head office showered me with awards and favours they gave stern warnings to my managerial colleagues not to try and copy my zany ways. One of me seemed to be enough for one company. For instance, a directive was issued that managers were not to go on stage and play records, but another directive said that this didn't apply to me. Thank goodness.

A high-ranking lady police officer came in one night and showed me the picture of an attractive girl who had run away from a remand home. 'Ah,' says I all serious, 'if she comes in I'll bring her back tomorrow but I'll keep her all night first as my reward.' The law lady, new to the area, was nonplussed. Back at the station she asked 'Is he serious?'

It is God's truth that the absconder came in that night. Taking her into the office I said, 'Run now if you want but you can't run for the rest of your life.' She listened to the alternative and agreed that I hand her over if she could stay at the dance, come home with me, and that I would promise to see her when they let her out. At 11.30 the next morning she was willingly presented to an astounded lady of the law The officeress was dissuaded from bringing charges against me by her colleagues, for it was well known that were I to go I would probably take half the station with me.

By now I had bought a nearly new Rolls Royce. This was made possible by selling my old strange one for a very high price and this was, in turn, made possible by giving one of my workers a substantial wage increase to pay his instalments. That way everyone was happy.

And now came the big break.

Into the hall wandered a Decca Records executive who was also a Radio Luxembourg disc jockey, Pat Campbell. In amazement he watched a packed floor dance to everything from rock and roll to the Peer Gynt Suite and low lights. An Irishman and receptive to atmosphere, he was instantly convinced that here was a new radio colleague. It took him six months to convince his London masters but finally they gave me a try.

At the time of the momentous decision I was in New York. Another good business prize from Mecca, it was my first time in America. Discovering that the cheapest room in the Waldorf Astoria hotel was just about within my stretch I had booked in at this millionaire's boarding house. All this worked wonders with the Luxembourg bosses as I must be a man of considerable substance to stay in such a gaff. A surprise telegram from England announced, 'Your radio show starting in three weeks. Please contact on return.'

One New York story first. My least expensive single room at the Waldorf was miles in the sky. Keenly anticipating watching American television I was chagrined to note that there was no telly in the room. The socket was there but obviously the telly had gone for repair. I smelt I could pull a stroke.

This fine hotel is justly proud of its good name so I singled out a friendly looking receptionist. Ignoring the fact he was working I launched into the 'nice place you've got here' routine. After a few minutes of wishing I'd drop dead the admirable chap puts down his pen to talk. The story that this once in a lifetime trip had cost me my entire roll interested him not at all because in the U.S.A. if you are skint they don't even see you: like you were just invisible. My ace card was that hotels in Britain were better because you could at least see TV. Stung to his national quick the clerk suggested I should switch on the set in my room. The news that my room had everything but a TV set destroyed him. The British equivalent would be to build a hotel without any toilets. With a mixture of national pride, company loyalty, my chance remark that he looked young to be the manager, my new receptionist friend took my key and by skilful accountancy gave me a whole suite on the fifth floor, for the same price. The gentleman deserves to prosper.

My first radio recording was due the day after I returned home. It wasn't to be just another radio show, as the great Warner Bros. film studios had decided to enter the pop record field and I was to host this European radio effort. The entire business was agog with the prospect and all waited eagerly for these smooth American sounds. People automatically presumed that Jimmy Savile was some guy with smooth transatlantic tones.

The consternation of the trade when some impossible Yorkshire voice announced 'Ello, welcome t' Warner Brothers Show' was quite dramatic.

Phone calls from the trade asked 'Who the hell was that on last night? You're joking' and suchlike. My professional embryo was saved by the listening figures. In the first three weeks they'd shot up from 600,000 to 2,300,000. As with the Mecca scene, nobody could argue with that business. After four weeks I had three radio shows and after three months I was doing five separate and different type pop shows every week. With an astronomical gross income of £300 a week it required some very heavy thinking to make sure I didn't go round the twist.

The term 'rat race' is oft used in the world of showbiz. The phrase actually describes a very simple structure. A young person is suddenly hurled into stardom and big money. It is a quite bewildering world and the new star thinks that tomorrow will be the same as today. Fashions change, there is much fiddling and if the new arrival is not good at business then he or she or they are plucked clean as a Christmas goose and slung on the heap. It is only a rat race when you're unsuccessful. By the time I arrived on the front doorsteps of Radio Luxembourg I was an expert wheeler-dealer, company politician and masterstroke-puller.

The first broadside that threatened my newfound and desirable world was a good showbiz baptism. Station policy was suddenly altered to become multi-lingual. All shows had to have German and French bits in them. This meant clumsy radio and loss of personal power. 'Great,' says I when told, 'about time I got chance to use my languages.' Assuring all of my seven language ability I pointed out that if I were able to knock off the programmes in the same time it would save them recruiting foreign personnel and not even interfere with their lunches and golf. A powerful inducement.

Whipping smartly off to a translator with a list of phrases and sentences I would need for this foreign pop talk I was ready for my new dimension by the following week. An admiring crowd of executives heard me suddenly and smoothly float into French and German and the new pro-grammes were dispatched for transmission. It had all been too easy and I viewed the forthcoming week with forboding.

Sure enough disaster struck. My translator happened to be an eighty-year-old German lady and there appeared to be no lingual equivalent to 'I'm gonna sock this one to you' and 'Hey, dig this you cats.' Whatever it was that came out on the air caused the German and French announcers in Luxembourg to fall down and have hysterics.

The big guns were levelled to blow me out of 'existence. Arriving at the studio I explained it all away. There were two sorts of German, the ordinary and the classical. I had just used the wrong one that's all. This week would be perfect, plus I'd throw in a bit of Spanish. It was agreed I'd have one more try. Again it was a load of bull but this time all the Spanish listeners were diverted to learn of some unfortunate feathered bird who had contrived to have a tree thrust up its arse. This was my translation of 'A bird in the hand is worth two in the bush!'

After two weeks of this lousy radio policy it was abandoned. I was bigger than ever and, to put it in its nicest sense, distrusted.

Once again my long suffering dance hall employers were faced with a Gordian situation. How could a manager be a disc jockey and a pop star earning £300 on his day off and still be a manager? For that was the way my Yorkshire logic had dictated it. To carry on, on all fronts, at the same time. All my showbiz work was crammed into one day, Thursday, my day off.

This incredible work load I carried for a year and a half. Towards the end of this unbelievable eighteen months I had added a weekly column in the *Sunday People* and Top of the Pops on TV. With the aid of this treble-headed media monster I was now going out to 40,000,000 people a week.

It was now a case of settling down until those vast numbers of people had known me long enough to be friends.

To be a pop star is very exciting. It can also kill you, cause you to commit suicide or plunge you into a mental turmoil that puts you beyond people. Working two main jobs at once helped me over the first hurdles. Needless to say the Leeds dance hall was busting at the seams. I had only to stand in the foyer for a minute and the passers-by would stop and stare. To live like this in a sort of fishtank was like living in a permanent circus. To be physically fit was a must.

A training programme was worked out which started at midnight. This comprised of a several mile run and was enthusiastically greeted by the more adventurous of my male dance hall staff. Our first effort was memorable. Fleeing through the darkened streets, the three tail-enders of our group were promptly apprehended by the law. Too out of puff to be coherent it was some time before they were let off the hook. The city soon became accustomed to exhausted young men legging through the night.

These training sessions were not without their fun and frights. One time I had set on a young giant of a minder who stood some six feet six. On his first run he was overcome with fatigue. Hailing a passing cab he demanded transporting to the all night café we used as base. Once inside the vehicle his body heat steamed up all the windows and the taxi man had to drive with his head hanging outside. On arrival at the café my giant worker tripped over the entrance step and crashed in headlong flight through the doors. Cries of panic came from within as this fiery, panting apparition, at an angle of forty-five degrees, charged through the tables and customers scattering all as the proverbial chaff. As it was 1 a.m. and several of the customers had been dozing, a lively scene ensued. My normally polite monster addressed himself to the terrified proprietor and explained he had tripped over the step and was one of my team. It actually came out in a series of gasps and hand motions and convinced all assembled that he was an escaped lunatic. The scene was calmed by the cab driver coming in for his money and explaining the story.

Have you ever gone into a shop and something odd has happened before you can open your mouth? On one of my trips to France I had walked into a shop to ask a price and there was a lady behind the counter. The counter was also the same height as my pelvic bone. Hand's in trouser pockets I leaned forward to speak, but before I could utter a word over-balanced and rocked back and forth, perfectly balanced by the hips. As I couldn't get my trapped hands out of my trouser pockets I was well stuck and the alarmed lady summoned her husband with loud Gallic cries. He levered me upright but as I couldn't speak French at the time all I could do was smile like Charlie Chaplin and bow out.

After six months at my part-time, Midas-touch radio job it was popularity poll time in the *New Musical Express*. I was astounded, really, to see that I had shot straight into eighth position. Never having been anything that people could vote for, it came as a shock. This was in the disc jockey section, and of the four big music papers I had made it into the charts of each one. The following year it was the no. 2 spot and then the no. 1. How dizzy are the heights from the top of the tree. It was all too splendid for words.

Now was the time for some real fun. Not that I went looking for fun, it just happened.

Travelling through Berkeley Square one morning a most super new Rolls, standing in Jack Barclay's famous showroom, caught my eye. Stopping the taxi and walking in was a matter of seconds. Making up my mind to buy it was a matter of minutes. Convincing the salesman that either he or I was not dreaming was another matter. As I have always tended to dress for convenience rather than fashion the man could be forgiven for looking askance at this figure dressed in a strange assortment of clothes and rounded off by no socks and fur bedroom slippers. Well known as I might be then among teenagers, adults had not the faintest idea who I was.

'How much?' said I, of the car.

'£7,500,' was the reply. It was only humouring me that I might leave quicker that made him reply at all.

'I'll have it. Deliver it to this address at eleven in the morning.' Scribbling my virtually unknown name and Mecca head office address on a bit of paper I made off in the cab. Needless to say at eleven the next morning no Rolls arrived. Nor did I really expect it to as I was now quite used to the strange life of never being taken seriously.

Having been transferred to the dance hall head office as assistant to the famous Eric Morley, this gave me a London secretary and it was she who phoned Jack Barclay's and asked, sweetly, where was the car for her boss. In a state of considerable agitato the salesman, convinced it was a hoax but afraid to risk it wasn't, jumped into this most magnificent vehicle and drove it round to Southwark Street. My office was so small that there was only room for one desk. As my secretary had to have something to lean on all day it was hers. All I had was a chair.

Writing out a cheque for £7,500 I requested that the car should be returned tomorrow at 11 a.m., ready for the road.

'Tomorrow?' croaked the salesman.

'Sure,' says I with a smile. 'That'll give you time to get the cheque cleared.'

How different it was on the morrow. Actually there was a terrible coincidence that I wouldn't have had happen for worlds. The joint chairman of Mecca was Carl Heimann for whom I had enormous respect, and I remember him in my prayers to this day. He had just purchased a second-hand Rolls from, I believe, Charles Clore, a gent with a few quid even in those days. This was delivered at 10.55. At 11.00, up drew behind my immaculate new one driven by a chauffeur in grey who stood to attention by the car. Every window of head office had heads hanging out to see one or the other. Out marched C. L. H. as we called him. He was taken aback by the two Rolls.

'Whose is that?' said he.

'It's Jimmy Savile's new one' was the doorman's reply.

'The bastard,' said C. L. H. But he smiled with it for he was an infinitely wise man who could see the inevitable.

So after ten years of life, love and training with that great company I just had to leave for it was an impossible situation to have a job at £25 a week and earn £15,000 a year on your day off. Running the two worlds side by side had been invaluable for the year and a half as it made sure I wouldn't overbalance as I went from one to the other.

My new world was a complete fairytale and it still is. Crazy, topsy-turvy, unreal, a social phenomenon of this century, and I love it.

Imagine what it is like to be able to do almost what you want. Fly to Australia? Buy an island? Have a thousand suits? It's all yours as long as you don't let it kill you.

Released from my seven-days-a-week job left me with masses of time.

The first thing was to sort out the Duchess, my mother. 'The Duchess' was my nickname for her and she was my life by the simple fact that there was no one else. It was our joint regret that my father was not alive to enjoy the halcyon days that were to come.

The first thing was to get her out of our old family house in Leeds. Whereas I would leave only when it was pulled down, big old houses are not good for seventy-year-old ladies. Think not that three score years and ten were a handicap for the Duchess. She had the energy of a teenager and could pleasure all night as often as the opportunity arose. My fortunes arrived in the nick of time for I had arrived home one day to find her within hours of death through ignored influenza and hypothermia. Three weeks in a private nursing home sorted that out and off we went. Bundling her into the car it was Scarborough first stop. That super seaside town has long been a magnet for those of us born in these Yorkshire acres. Driving up to my favourite view on the clifftop Esplanade it suddenly occurred to me that the apartments overlooking it were now within my reach. With my usual luck there was a choice one available. It was negotiated in a twinkling and within seven days of stopping to look at the view, the Duchess was installed.

One day I might write the story of my mother. She was quite impossible in, of course, the most lovable way. A few stories here will suffice.

We have always been a close family, my brothers Vince and John plus four sisters Mary, Marjorie, Joan and Chrissie, but of course the Duchess would bore the pants off anyone who would listen to her tales of my exploits.

She invariably got the details back to front and all mixed up but this trifling inaccuracy bothered her not at all. Nothing bothered her at all. It was a waste of time to correct her as the following tale will tell.

Sitting in our super seafront flat one day she was holding forth to some of her lady pals. I was reading. One of the ladies had mentioned the Post Office Tower in London. 'Oh yes,' said the Duchess, 'Jimmy opened that.'

Now it's a known fact that the Queen took that particular job on. 'No sweetheart,' said I, 'the Queen opened it. I just hold the record for running up the steps.'

(Some time previously I'd mentioned this particular feat to which the Duchess had replied at the time, over her eternal knitting, 'You'll hurt yourself doing silly things like that.')

'Nonsense,' says she at this correction, 'you told me you opened it.' And then to explain to her friends my interruption she said, 'He did really', adding the silencer of all time, 'he forgets things you know.'

What could you do with an impossible girl like that other than love her more than your own life?

Her naivety was monumental. About to go off on a trip to Spain she trots to the doctors. 'No Mrs Savile, you won't need anything, you're remarkably fit.' That wasn't good enough for her. She needed pills of some sort or the trip would lose its flavour. Surrendering, the doctor suggested she buy some water-sterilizing tablets in case the local Spanish water was off. Satisfied, the Duchess left him and marched to the chemists. It was full but my mother was small and appeared at the counter.

'Yes Mrs Savile?' asked the chemist.

'I want some sterilization pills,' quoth the Duchess.

This brought the shop to a standstill. The chemist coughed and leaned over the counter.

'Er, who for?' he said.

'Me,' announced the Duch.

Chemists are not used to being confronted by eighty-year-old ladies who fear they may become pregnant.

'You,' croaked the startled man.

'I'm going to Spain,' announced the Duchess grandly, 'and the doctor has advised that I take some sterilization pills.'

The shop collapsed and the chemist closed his eyes. My impossible darling explained to this obviously idiot man.

'He says the water may be contaminated—'

'WATER sterilizing tablets,' hollered the chemist.

The shop erupted into hysteria. She got the tablets, for which he would take no payment. True to her implacable nature she was greatly incensed, later, as I told her the facts of life.

CHAPTER FIVE

At that period, with time to spare, it was not long before fate once again steered me into a new way of life. The hospital world. The 'I'm backing Britain' campaign was upon us. Looking for something non-political and non-sectarian to do made me turn to voluntary hospital work. Leeds Infirmary is close to my house so as I already had a working arrangement with them to do the odd patients' broadcast I spoke to my friend, the head porter Charles Hullighan. 'How about me as a porter, two days a week for one month?' This novel idea was put before the board who said, 'Why not?' By now a national figure, my arrival for duty took the fancy of the media and they were there in force. Plus the chairman of the board, Sir Donald Kaberry.

With much activity all about I was solemnly handed over to an experienced porter from the X-ray department, Joe Tyrer. Followed by this retinue, and dressed in virginal white, I wheeled my first patient into the department for treatment.

For any person who thinks beyond the end of their nose, hospital work is a marvellous job: providing one can manage on the not so grand basic pay. To me, as a voluntary worker, it soon became obvious that I had stumbled on yet another way of life. My original month went by in a flash and it was by mutual consent that I just 'keep going'. At the time of this writing it's my seventh working year at Leeds Infirmary.

Story telling is one of my useful medical therapies and patients of different age groups want to know different things. 'What is Elvis really like?' 'Is it true you worked for a month with the Beatles?' 'What is Prince Philip like.' 'Did you really meet Pope John?'

But my goodness, hasten not, flying pen, or we shall finish without explaining these stories in their proper order.

It was probably the greatest ever thrill for the Duchess when I took her to Rome for a sort of private audience with the late, great, Pope John. In my travels I'd made the acquaintance of a big time priest who was based in that city of seven hills. Certainly he could get me two invitations to a private affair in the Vatican. I dropped the news on the Duchess one morning at breakfast. 'Don't be silly,' was her comment. She never ever got used to the idea that I could cause unusual things to happen, hence her life of initial doubt and subsequent amazement to any given circumstance.

It took the air hostess to convince her that the aircraft was flying to Rome and not Jersey. Such a time we had. From the Colosseum to the Catacombs I marched her over the face of this beautiful city. After some days a messenger arrived at our hotel with hand-graven invites to the Vatican. The Duchess, in Mephistophilesian black from head to foot, looked fit for a king's funeral.

Our arrival at the Vatican coincided with a turn-out of some considerable thousands of the equally faithful. Our invitations were for a special reception of diplomatic persons but it was impossible to find out exactly where to go. The Duchess, in a frenzy, brandished her card under the nose of everyone who looked official. Neither of us understanding Italian lent these interviews a lively exchange. My frail five foot female roundly cursed all who could not produce Pope John immediately, let alone the route to him. It was as frustrating as a football fan having a ticket for a seat in the director's box at Wembley and finding himself on the wrong end of 100,000 people.

With the Duchess hanging on to my coat I forced my way into the main body of the church. We had just admitted defeat against the crowd when there was a great commotion, pushing and applause. Carried on the shoulders of several strong men Pope John, sitting on a light throne, was carried towards us on the way to the altar. It couldn't have worked better and I'd never get another chance so I waved furiously, at the same time switching the Duchess from behind me to in front. The great man caught my wave and I pointed down to my, by now, transfixed mother. He was passing only six feet away and, God be praised, made the sign of the cross towards us. Some could argue that it was not much of a recognition for our journey and effort but we didn't feel it that way. It was two tired pilgrims that made it back to the hotel and the engraved invitations, never used but never mind, are among her treasure papers in Scarborough.

Seeing the Duchess had seen the Pope I decided it was about time I saw Elvis. At that time Elvis was about as approachable as the Dalai Lama. No one in England could really claim to have met up and socialized with him but I reckoned that Hollywood couldn't be any more difficult than St Peter's Square. So there I was, at 40,000 feet, heading over the North Pole towards California: with only one possible phone number where I could get information as to his whereabouts and clutching a gold disc for 1,200,000 sales of 'It's now or never' that I was going to use as a passport, it looked like being an exciting trip.

California, to someone from the moors of Yorkshire, is a contender for the Garden of Eden. Oranges on trees is definitely stuff that wall posters are made of. On the tops of Ilkley Moor only the heather bobs its head. The sight of a California hill covered with the uniform bobbing heads of donkey pumps, sucking oil from the depths, was a silencer. Gleaming cars and the gleaming bodies of beach girls made the head turn and I felt it officially criminal that the age of consent in that admirable state is eighteen. It really is unfair because everyone knows that everything matures quicker in the sunshine.

The morning after my arrival I phoned my precious number which turned out to be the Elvis office. Sounding quite casual, I said I had a gold presentation disc for Elvis so where could I bring it. As it happens he was filming at the Paramount Studios so would I take it round and give it to Colonel Tom Parker. The taxi got me there twenty minutes late. Through the incredible studio lot and on to a dark film set. The unmistakable figure of the Colonel hove into view.

'If you're the guy from England, you're late' he barked.

'Sorry about that,' says I, 'the traffic was a bit heavy over the last mile.'

The Colonel looked me over. 'Stay with me,' was his order.

Let me explain the quite unusual Colonel Tom Parker. He used to round up stray dogs in the street. Always a showman he went on to sell foot-long sausages in rolls on the fairground. Money was short so he would cut the sausages into bits, with only one end sticking out of the bread roll. When the customers complained of the almost total lack of sausage the Colonel would look over the counter on to the floor. There in the dirt was a trampled sausage. The customer would accept that he had dropped it out of the bread and the Colonel would not, of course, mention that before his stall opened for the day he had the foresight to toss a couple of foot-long sausages into the dirt. So, as an old-time fairground man, the Colonel was no mug. He was a character all the time, not just when anyone was looking. Therefore, as he suspected I was also a character, he felt I was worthy of closer inspection.

Lugging the gold disc we moved farther into the football-ground size studio.

'Fetch the boy,' barked the Colonel.

An aide hurried away. Suddenly out of the gloom walked Elvis.

Let me now explain about El.

My actual desire to see him face to face was not motivated by his singing. Good voice that he has when he has a mind to really sing, it has always been Nat King Cole, Sinatra, Ella and Tony Bennett for me. No, it was just to examine the incredible Elvis charisma that carries right round the world and gets millions of people at it. When you are in the company of someone really great there is something very, very different about them. Not easy to explain, one just senses that something that looks normal radiates to strange effect.

For instance, I experienced the same feeling the first time I helped load an unexploded bomb on to a wooden bomb-disposal ship of the Royal Navy; a sort of crinkly feeling that makes it difficult to talk as easily as one normally does. The first time a Britisher gets introduced to a member of the Royal Family he also gets just a bit tongue-tied. Afterwards you can think of a million things you could have said.

So, there was the great Elvis and it was all very super. Miracle upon miracles, the Col called for a photographer who shot several frames of all of us together plus El and me alone. In those days such a scoop was about the equivalent of kissing the Queen under the mistletoe. After a few minutes' chat El was called back to work and I had carefully avoided the pitfall question of when he was coming to Britain. Small talk after such a long journey made me an in person as far as the Col was concerned and this opened the door for an incredible few days, and several subsequent trips.

One never argued or questioned the Colonel. At 7.30 one morning I was awakened by a phone call from him. 'A car will collect you in twenty minutes. Don't touch any door handles anywhere.'

On the dot, up rolls a Caddi limousine. Rushing into the foyer the chauffeur opened the swing doors of my boarding house, the Beverly Hilton. Driving downtown I was ushered into a big hotel the name of which I forget. Not a word had been spoken by the driver and I didn't know what was expected of me. All I realized was the Colonel was up to his practical tricks on someone. It turned out to be a breakfast with a fabulously rich team of guys. Halfway through the silent meal the Colonel suddenly said to me, 'I'm sorry Elvis can't do that English job, your Lordship.'

Ah, that was it. In the trade it's called a 'wind up' which means you wind someone up with a fictitious situation.

Knock for knock I answered, 'That's O.K. Colonel, but a million pounds is a lot of money and a private 707 costs a goodly dollar.'

Money talk has a strange effect on American businessmen. With noses twitching like the Bramham Moor hounds' the other breakfast guests looked me over for a take-on. The bait had been thrown and they took it good.

'I might give you someone else,' murmured the Colonel.

We all got up to leave and one of the guests pretended to show me something in a showcase. Quick as a flash he produced a visiting card and hissed, 'Phone me, I can get you anyone in this country.'

Back in our limousine the Col roared with laughter. 'Greedy bastard,' says he. 'That guy's got 1,000 million dollars and I ain't never been able to take him before.' Everything was fair game for practical jokes for him, and I made a perfect double act, being quick on the uptake.

His dear lady wife was ill in a nursing home so round we went. After ten minutes in her private room the Colonel had an idea. 'Get out of bed,' says he to his surprised lady, 'and Jimmy will get in. We'll call the nurse and ask what the pills are doing to you. You can hide in the cupboard.'

'I will not,' expostulated his missus. And she meant it. Colonel Parker's face dropped and he looked at me, his new partner, for a way out. So I lay down on the floor.

'Call the nurse,' says I. 'Ask for some water, ignore me and drink it yourself.'

His face lit up. In came the nurse who jumped a mile at seeing me stretched out. Back in with a glass of water which the Col drank with great relish. Out she went, ignoring me but muttering, 'Everybody's crazy round here.' Which I suppose we were.

The sunshine and fun days went like a dream and it was back to Britain for me.

I was much touched later that year by a gesture from the Colonel. I had won the no. 1 disc jockey award and went to the Empire Pool to collect it before 10,000 people. For the first time in pop history, Elvis, winner of the Top Male Vocalist section, had sent a voice tape thanking his legions of fans. 'Listen to it,' said Maurice Kinn, editor of the *New Musical Express*, 'there's a surprise for you at the end.'

Sure enough, after thanking his fans, Elvis carried on 'and we were very pleased to have Jimmy Savile with us in Hollywood this year.'

Maurice had the tape put on a disc which I still have today.

For anyone who is business minded, the incredible multi-million dollar Elvis enterprise is run by only two people, the Colonel, and a super gentle gentleman Tom Diskin, plus an occasional secretary. Surely the world's smallest team for the world's largest pop industry.

Released now, as I was, from the day to day executive work from Mecca Ltd and with my voice and name becoming more well known nationally, these were the beautiful springtime days. Let me clarify that. Having not done very much television meant that I could walk through a railway station or department store unrecognized by all. Therefore one lived the best of both worlds. All the money one needed (I was earning about £500 a week) plus the complete mobility of a normal person. Hence it was the springtime of a career that was soon to put me into the full summer glare of a publicity which, with my distinctive hairstyle, made me the easiest recognizable man in the country, front or back!

My ten years with a big company had turned me into businessman par excellence and also company politician of a decidedly foxy nature. It is my theory in any given executive job it works out at ten per cent actually doing the job and ninety per cent of the time juggling the internal company intrigues. For pure simplicity and enjoyment of work, picking potatoes or emptying dustbins are among the top jobs. Having done both, I know.

Being in the unique position of having plenty of both money and time brought me to yet another fork in the path of life. Having developed into a teetotaller, non-gambler and non-smoker, except for cigars which one doesn't inhale, was another stroke of personal good fortune. Most of my pop colleagues would loon and quaff the night away but I was well content with my newfound ease and the company of the skint or just unlucky. My intimate knowledge of business and people turned me into a sort of citizens' advice bureau. The small hotel I used when in London soon became a haven for young men and pop groups who wanted a word of advice or suggestion or just a chat.

One such group presented itself at my door. Earnest and solemn of face, they were down from Wales but things were not going right. Several discussions we had at all odd hours. They would tell me their progress and I would suggest a course of action. It started things going the right way and the caterpillar of Tommy Scott and the Senators turned into the world-beater winged wonder of our own Tom Jones. I would never make claim to be responsible for anyone's success but when a top man has time to talk or eat with new arrivals it gives a tremendous boost to the morale of the beginners.

At the time I was playing the records of one of the first real long-hair groups, on Radio Luxembourg. Their first disc didn't make it. I was definitely the only disc jockey to play the second one. An executive from their record company came in to the studio brandishing a photo of the group. 'Have you seen these layabouts you're championing?' says he. The picture showed five young men standing by some railings. 'Sure,' says I, 'we keep with them, they have a good sound.' Keep with them I did, and just as well. The group was the Rolling Stones. Nobody argued with me after that.

Two lads came to see me. One was a singer but wanted to sing soul music. The other was his manager who felt a trip to the Godfather was advisable. 'Do you want to sing soul or do you want to eat?' was my question. I was lying in bed at the time. 'Eat,' says the manager half. 'Right, so you sing little boy stuff and smile as you do it.' The singing half didn't go much on my suggestion but just the same did as I said. A year later I got a letter from him. It was written on a flight to America. 'Dear Jimmy, I never thanked you for the advice which I stuck to. I'm just going to collect my first gold disc.' He was to collect many more for his 'little boy' tunes because he was Hermann of Hermits fame. Real name Peter Noone, and a world-class entertainer now.

I always was, and still am, attracted and fascinated by the phenomenon of the pop star success and hysteria. Invited by the late Brian Epstein to compère a three week long Beatles Christmas Show at Hammersmith Odeon I claim to be the only member of the show that stood glued to the floor in the wings during every minute of their twice nightly contributions.

For anyone interested in people like I was, it was a most incredible three weeks. A packed theatre in total screaming accord with their idols on stage gives off a charge relative to electro kinetic energy. It consumes all whom it affects. Most human beings are prey to some strong feeling. A dislike of snakes or spiders perhaps. Claustrophobia or agoraphobia. Sufferers know all too well these strong emotive things. Beatle mania, or Stones, Monkees, Osmonds—all collect their followers. Religions, cults, isms, all peoples have strange habits to other people.

Behind the scene on this Beatles show was marvellous.

We enjoyed, and still do, considerable mutual respect.

Their dressing room was always open to me and just as I was content to sit around and listen with Elvis and the Colonel so I was with the Beatles. Let me use these guys to look at this incredible world of what can happen if you are a pop success.

In their own way they are very level-headed. From their background, a strong touch of cynicism makes them intolerant of humbug. Suddenly plunged into a world of being not only millionaires but world-wide idols and sex symbols didn't actually change them all that much, but by golly it did change the rest of the world towards those four lads. The world they knew, filled with normal people, had disappeared. In its place was a world where only buses and cars looked the same. People reacted from screaming violently, hustling for favours, to being enviously offensive.

The Beatles got into big trouble for walking out of a reception for them at the British Embassy in Washington. 'Disgusting', 'A disgrace to the country' was the verdict of most of the public at home. The truth of the matter was related to me by Brian Epstein who took care of them there. The boys hadn't wanted to go, knowing it would develop into a free for all. The packed guests at the reception were not at all after the Beatles' autographs but for most of them it was a big thing that they could take these same autographs back for diplomatic and important industrialists' children. The pushing and jostling that the lads had prophesied started but these were not good-natured teenage jostlers. These were important adult ones and several of them carrying a fair quantity of Her Britannic Majesty's free booze. Having been in similar type circumstances I can tell you it gets quite unlovely. It was not surprising that the boys pulled up stumps and left. Nor was it the fault of the embassy. Such places are not mentally geared to cope with the illogical pop phenomena. It was just one of those things, but manna from heaven for the newspaper lads.

Being the only one in the theatre with free access to their dressing room it fell to my lot that only I could intercede for special cases. For instance, a father had travelled from Buffalo in the U.S. to Hammersmith Odeon with his two small daughters. Such was Beatle mania. They had seen the show and had made it to the stage door. A private look at the Beatles was out of the question but the doorkeepers summoned me as a first and last hope. Taking the two small ladies by the hand I marched into the lads' room. 'Say good evening,' I commanded. The four boys did so, willingly. Out I marched with my two transfixed charges.

Such actions earned me the nickname from the boys of Doctor Do-Good. Many deserving cases of all shapes and sizes did I appear with and had no trouble at all. Except the last lot. Two teenage girls they were. Once again the door-keepers had come to me with their story. The two girls had travelled a considerable distance and didn't have tickets for the show. What money they had was spent on a bouquet of flowers for the Beatles. What could I do? I spelled it out clearly. 'I'll take you into the dressing room. Put the flowers on the table, say good evening to the lads, and out we go.'

This was far more than the girls had dreamed of and they promised that all would be well. Alas, the sight of John, Paul, George and Ringo actually sitting on two settees taking it easy was too much. Everything happened at once. One girl emitted a piercing scream and fell to the floor. The other called for Paul, as with her dying breath, and hurled herself on the startled star. Paul made his escape by climbing over John and it was all a terrible mêlée accompanied by the continued screaming from the fan on the floor. The arrival of Mal and Mel, the Beatles' roadies, and friends added to the general commotion. The two girls, all arms, legs and Knickers, were bundled out and I dissolved with laughter. 'Ah well Jim,' said Paul, sorting out the general damage, 'we won't be seeing much of you then.' He didn't really mean it

77

of course and I was still allowed my Doctor Do-Good routine.

About this time I got a phone call from B.B.C. TV. 'My name is Johnny Stewart and I'm starting a programme called Top of the Pops. Will you be the first disc jockey on the show?' And so ended the springtime of my pop career. Here then started the 100 degree summer with no clouds to cover the burning brilliance of total recognition by, eventually, nearly all this country's 53 million people.

Had I, at that point, retired, emigrated or got married I could have lived out the rest of my days content with my successes, awards and even savings. Being fairly frugal and only me and the Duchess to feed there was no real need for me to earn more big lumps of money. Such tranquillity was not meant for me. Top of the Pops became a way of life that branded me as some sort of nutter.

Not wanting to get any farther up any tree, each day became a holiday. Having a laugh, at no one else's expense but mine, was the motivating force behind all my strange clothes and antics. I once did a five minute inset into the show hanging upside down from a rope tied round my feet. In the studio we all had a laugh but in millions of homes people said, 'What for hang upside down, he is a nut.' My legitimate business colleagues would say, 'Standing on his head I feel safe, standing on his feet I worry he takes over my business.'

Let me dwell on the phenomenon of being famous. I've not really had much time to think of it before. When I was ordinary I used to go to a turkish bath in Leeds. Sitting in the steam room would be an assortment of glistening, naked men. I used to wonder, why is that naked body rich and that one not? They look so alike just now. It was easy to see why a rugby player was a rugby player. God had just dished out a heavier or more muscular body than the norm. But why should one naked body command respect from another and what was the charisma that put one man well above his neighbour when we all sweated the same. I searched long for the answer. Time was one factor I came up with. It was necessary for a man to be successful by degrees, over a period of time, without any slip-ups along the way. Therefore patience seemed to be a vital thing. Without patience there comes exasperation. Exasperation could cause you to step back instead of inching forward. Lying on the smooth beds afterwards I would reflect that if one kept going one became more credible each day. As my progress was snail slow at the time it was obviously going to take me ages to reach a command situation. Time therefore was important and effort secondary. Such a theory was apt for the situation, whereupon I would fall into a deep sleep. Purely as a statistical postscript if I slept for two hours, during that period several hundred people would die violent deaths, somewhere else, so I wasn't all that bad a judge.

These days there are many famous and easy to recognize persons. Newscasters are as familiar as your next-door neighbours. Politicians are well enough known to do impersonations of. When therefore I say that to be famous is incredible fun, this applies more to me than possibly them. People can vociferously and unpleasantly disagree with politicians when recognized, and the public can gape at the familiar face of a newscaster but would never laugh, shake his hand or wave at him from passing cars. The effect I have on people in public places is varied, often strange but never unhappy. This is due simply to the fact that I've never had to sell anybody anything. With me life was always candy floss.

When Winston Churchill died the queues to pay their respects were fantastic. I went down but it was impossible to get in unless you had three hours to spare. There is a monument to him and I bow to his memory, in human terms not political.

When I die it will make the national press but there will

be no queue to see me, or monument. This suits me because yesterday's fun should be forgotten in the search for today's fun. History has it that people with the power to amuse fail sometimes to achieve their own happiness and on occasions take their own life. Therefore I was favoured by God that the good times I have obviously entertain or mildly intrigue people with time to spare from the toil of life.

For instance, where would you see a dust cart being chased by screaming girls?

This unlikely event took place in Scarborough. Doing some training for a forthcoming wrestling bout I bumped into the lads that empty the bins round my flat. 'Come and work an hour with us,' they urged. 'Humping the bins is good training.' So on went the old clothes and it was off to work on the back step of the dust cart. A great time we had and eventually finished up on the seafront, emptying the bins of the arcades. A sack on my head like a monk's cowl hid my telltale locks. Some schoolgirls on a day trip were idling near a passageway. 'Good Lord, that dustman's the spit and image of Jimmy Savile,' said one. Out of curiosity they waited for my loaded return. Slinging the refuse into the motor cart the bin took my disguise sack as well. 'Ahhhh,' screamed the young ladies. 'It is him.' And forward they charged with a passion that my idol Winston would have applauded. With great presence of mind the lads leapt aboard the back step and off we roared down the front. Surprised holidaymakers stood aghast at the unlikely scene of forty fine-bodied young girls running, with shrill cries, after a dust cart. The explanation that Jimmy Savile was one of the dustmen brought back forth much of 'whatever will he get up to next'.

CHAPTER SIX

There have been TV shows which try, for once in a lifetime, to give a member of the public the reality of a long-time-held off-beat desire. Imagine then a life where almost every off-beat desire was easily possible.

Would you like to pull a ten-ton tram full of people steered by a Lord Mayor? How about jumping into a snake-pit with thirty Russell vipers for which there is no known serum? Or flying in the lead aircraft of a near supersonic aerobatic team? Having enjoyed these three doubtful delights, let me relive them.

The tram story was a case of how to succeed by doing your homework first. It was the Isle of Man where I was doing my weekly observation on the methods of my hypnotist friend Josef. Looking around for a little stroke to pull on the people I wondered how difficult it would be to actually pull one of the horse-drawn trams that run the length of the fine promenade of Douglas. These patient horses plod the seafront daily, fastened on to a single or double deck tram carrying collections of holidaymakers. As the promenade is quite flat there's no undue effort needed from the beasts. It occurred to me that if I were to swop places with a horse it could be quite a stunt, and a laugh. Not wishing to rupture myself in front of the possible multitude, a little rehearsal was advisable but secrecy was vital.

At 2 a.m. one dark morning I tapped on the door of the tram sheds. Lights inside had told me that a night maintenance man was doing his nocturnal thing. The door opened a crack, for who but a drunk would knock at such an ungodly hour?

Instant recognition has its advantages and in a twinkling

I was inside and shaking hands with the nightwatchman. Explaining my plot, and desire, a single deck tram was unbraked and turned out to be surprisingly easy to push or pull. The execution would be easy so all I needed was to create the reason. The next night saw me socializing in the seafront casino. Before the night was out a casino boss had been provoked enough to bet me £50 I couldn't pull a full tram the length of the prom. As no one had done it before it seemed a safe bet. I had to fly back to London to do Top of the Pops but promised the tram spectacle for the following Friday.

During the week, unknown to me, argument had reigned to some degree as to the physical possibility of such a feat. My arrival back on the island put me into the centre of a fever of doubt and anticipation. Seven p.m. of that fine summer evening was the time I announced for the big pull. At six I was at the stables and fitted myself out with a horse collar, it being the most comfortable, logical way to work. On arrival at the tram sheds, a fine old to-do was going on.

Permission to pull, as it were, had been given by the transport authority, and a driver, or, more exact, a brakeman had been allocated. The unheralded arrival of the Mayor and Mayoress caused a small flap and when His Worship announced that he would personally be the driver, this caused a much larger flap. The original driver, stung, uttered loud cries of protest but was summarily silenced by the Mayor who revealed that, in his early working days, he too had been a brakeman so that was that.

About 20,000 people were lining the route, which wasn't bad for a word-of-mouth stunt. Came the moment of truth when, complete with big boots and horse collar, I took the strain. Dear God, the tram seemed screwed to the floor and a shot of panic speared my heart.

What I hadn't taken into account was that the first fifty yards from the sheds to the prom was up an ever so slight gradient. The first effort needed was immense and I thought the veins in my neck would burst. Urged on by the cries of the multitude and the unthinkable fact that I might fail, first one foot then another found purchase on the floor. Slowly the equipage moved on into the evening sunlight and, sweating like a tap, me and my suddenly million-ton tram breasted the rise. Up on the front and all became easy, or comparatively so as I still had a mile and a half to pull. After a while, my heart and other vital organs returned to their normal resting places.

An unforeseen complication now turned up. As I was walking and pulling at a quite steady pace and it was a nice evening, most of the 20,000 spectators decided that they would stroll along with me. This succeeded in bringing all wheeled life on the prom to a halt. An even further complication nearly got my head stove in. The first tram we saw coming in the opposite direction was pulled by a venerable old nag for whom life had just been one long drag. Justifiably alarmed at the approach of such a horde of humans the animal gave a loud snort and hove to.

I felt it fitting to call a friendly greeting to my stable companion. 'Hello brother horse' was my contribution to equestrian equality. It would appear, on reflection, that Isle of Man horses do not converse when about their daily ploy.

Several things happened at once.

The noble shire beast reared up on its back legs and uttered a shrill cry of fear. The Mayor promptly applied the brakes and near dislocated my two arms and neck simultaneously. The driver of the tram with the rearing beast in the shafts, not to be outdone, reared up also and added his contribution of hoarse cries to this by now lively mêlée. The crowd cheered this wild-west spectacular and I narrowly avoided being decapitated by the flailing hooves of this Wyatt Earp steed. Statesmanlike action was called for. Shouting for the Mayor to unleash the brake, I did another up-the-incline effort and broke into a trot.

The five hundred yards from the happening to the harbour was a scene to remember. Me, the tram and its occupants, about a dozen policemen who were looking after the Mayor, and some thousands of people all clipped along at about seven miles an hour. The crowd, taken by a fine madness, ran and laughed and cheered until we ran out of tramline. It only then dawned on all of us that there was now no horse to pull the tram all the way back to the sheds.

My offer to oblige was not taken up. 'Get rid of him first,' ordered a police inspector. 'Then we can try and get some order out of this madhouse.' So, complete with horse collar, I was bundled into a police car and whisked off. The £50 was duly paid up and sent to a local charity, and all in all it was a pleasant change for a pleasant evening.

The snakepit story is one that even now gives me the horrors. Having been invited by the management of Woburn Safari Park to do a visit for my famous Savile's Travels radio show, it was to be my first sight of animals in the wild. The men and women who work on these parks make danger look easy. My first effort was to advance on a herd of dozing rhinoceros to have my picture taken with them. All around, the cars of the visitors circled constantly. Accompanied by a minder I tramped over the grass carrying a rifle in best big game tradition. There were no bullets in it. The rhinos, short-tempered and unpredictable, were lying down in a bunch. Up to that point the thought of fear had never crossed my mind. Suddenly my minder started to say, 'There boy, there boy' in a sort of singsong voice.

'What's up?' says I, breaking out into a sweat.

'They can get funny at times,' replied my fearless companion.

My sweat turned ice cold and my forward pace slowed considerably. I added several 'there boys' to his for good measure and several Hail Marys for even better measure. There is something unique about staring a wild beast straight in the eye.

84

'Scratch its belly,' said the Safari boss.

'It might be a lady one and object,' was my shaky reply.

All this time a photographer with a long-range lens was recording the confrontation. Visitors' cars had slowed to a crawl, marvelling at the courage of the modern disc jockey. The truth of it was that I was petrified, and I'm sure you would have been too.

It had to happen. One of the beasts got up. Three tons of rhino plus magnificent horn squared up to the human intruders.

'Just walk away quietly,' murmured my pal.

I swear to God it was the longest walk of my life. Back in the safety of our car my insides turned to jelly.

'Do we have a loo round here?' I asked, lighting a cigar with a great show of unconcern. Loo first and a cup of tea next put me back to square one.

Half a day of wandering about the park collecting interviews and keeping well away from any more rhino-type trauma and it came to me that I hadn't seen the snakes. Now snakes I cannot stand, not even the harmless grass ones, but, like some of my non-courageous ilk, am fascinated to watch them through glass. They have a genuine snakepit at Woburn. Introduced to the two gentlemen snake-handlers we peered into the circular concrete well. Lying on the bottom were two coiled reptiles. 'Russell vipers' I was informed.

Some thirty visitors lined the top wall of the pit which was about eight feet deep. A small moat of running water bubbled round the outside circumference of the bottom. A thought, the like of which will be my eventual undoing, crossed my mind. If only somehow I could get the snakes hissing into my microphone, what a super finish it would make to the programme. The mike lead was only four feet long and the snakes could be the type that went to kip for a month. However, two snakes plus two handlers armed with

metal pronged sticks would surely keep me safe were I to
venture into the noisome depths. It was too good to miss.

'Can the three of us jump in and wake 'em up?' I said.

The handlers looked at me. 'Are you serious?'

'Sure,' says I, thinking of nought but the dare-devil end-
product. In a twinkling they were over and down and so
was I.

As is so often the case in my incredible career I had not
taken all the possibilities into consideration. For instance,
having seen only two snakes it never ever occurred to me
that there could be more. That which from the safety of the
top had looked like, so I thought, food dishes turned out,
Sweet Jesus, to be two snake houses. The reason that only
two snakes were visible was that the inverted bowls were full
of heaving masses of these formidable reptiles. My frights
with the rhinos were as nothing compared to my first thirty
seconds down that pit as the lads flipped the covers off the
kipping coils. Think me not crude if I describe my condition
as shitsville, for shitsville it was and no mistake.

The handlers were busy on two tasks. One was to dis-
entangle the mass of snakes and hurl the surprised reptiles
into the water trough. The other, far more important task
to my mind, was to keep the venomous things from getting
back out and biting us.

'How many are there?' was my panic-stricken question.

'Thirty-six,' was the terse reply.

To the visitors, now thick round the top, this was a spectacle without parallel. 'Behind you, behind you,' they cried
until I spun round like a top.

At this point let me explain something. Several days prior
to my visit, the daily papers had carried a near-death story
of one of the very snake-handlers who was now defending
me, who had been inadvertently bitten by a Russell viper of
this particular tribe. There would appear to be no cure for
this venom and the lad had been in the intensive care unit

for some days. He had, miraculously, lived. In an effort to keep sane in this horror situation of all time I shouted to him, 'Which was the one that bit you?' Like big joke.

His reply brought me a quick touch of rigor mortis. 'That was a baby one only two weeks old. There's no second chance with these grown-up bastards.'

His pal summed up the situation perfectly. 'Let's go Jim.' Of such is the human mind when terrified to paralysis that it had never occurred to me to escape.

With a spring of Olympic proportions I took off, my five pound tape-recorder hampering me not a jot, closely followed by my companions. We hung over the inside of the pit like three victims on the death hooks of the walls of an ancient Moroccan city. Back on dry land as it were, I was totally spent. I suspected it was not entirely all in a day's work for the two lads either. With legs of rubber and ice cold from the reaction, I once again went into my famous loo and tea routine. Such an experience is not advisable and most positively not repeatable.

Why do people do things like that? Let me try and work it out. It's all to do with the chemistry of memory and consequence. One forgets the memory of being afraid and one ignores the possibility of consequence. Disaster or divine deliverance is the outcome. Once again the Good Lord had given me the cold shoulder from joining His ranks. I have every reason to believe I may never die.

And now, a confession. Listeners to Savile's Travels on the radio went cold as they listened to the hissing of thirty-six Russell vipers. Forget it, it was me hissing in different keys after. It wasn't exactly cheating because I had actually gone through the tremendous experience and come to think of it I can't remember any of the snakes hissing. Maybe those ones don't. Anyway, I was damned if I was going through all that for no sound effects. So I did it myself.

By now, trying to live a normal life was impossible. It was

87

a strange world. As I was game for anything, invitations for everything came tumbling in. All of the written ones I could refuse because just getting out of bed got me into enough scrapes.

'Would you consider opening our Air Day at Brawdy?' Thus spake the clean-cut guy in the sergeants' mess at the Royal Marines, Lympstone, training centre. An innocent and exciting request as I love watching aeroplanes and here was the prospect of a grandstand seat.

Exciting it was to be, grandstand most certainly, but innocent, never. It started off that I was to arrive at the airfield, in Pembrokeshire, in a small Tiger Moth plane. That would have been innocent enough. However, at that time Brawdy was the home of the Fleet Air Arm daredevils, the Diamonds. This was an aerobatic jet team similar to the Red Devils of the R.A.F. The Navy fliers used full-blooded Hunter fighter bombers that went terribly fast.

'If you come up with us,' said the clean-cut guy, 'and you don't black out, throw up, or die, we'll make you Diamond Six.' There were five of them already.

I always find it most easy to agree, and shudder to think what life would have been like for me had I been born a girl.

Arriving on the camp a day early the doctor was soon peering down my ears and up my nose: favourite areas, it appears, for supersonic damage. As it turned out, a cork up the rectum would have been much better. Passed as fit and fastened into an ejector-seat simulator I was hurled on to a floor full of mattresses to teach me how to proceed should I want to part myself from a failing jet plane. At eight the next morning, before the crowds had started to arrive, it was time for my testing trip. Now that the moment of truth had arrived I welcomed back the two conditions of my repeated dice-with-death escapades, a repeated swallowing and breathlessness.

Five silent jet fighters standing just off the runway on a

fine morning is a beautiful sight. A sort of aerodynamic poetry. Swallowing like a camel and breathing like after a furious love tussle I was introduced into the co-pilot seat of what was to be the lead aircraft, by a ground technician. He saved my life but he didn't know it. It was like this. The difference between simulating and actuality can be a little or a lot. I had done everything for safety's sake but had not tasted the quite incredible and almost indescribable gravitational pull to the earth. The dreaded G force. A simple hydraulic feature. If your body leaves the earth at sufficient speed it causes your liquids, like blood, to rush to your feet and legs. All the blood downstairs means none upstairs which is O.K. if you keep your brains in your feet. No oxygen carrying blood to the brain and it's grey-out, blackout, or goodbye Mum!

Firstly, I was not wearing a G suit. These strange garments, under stress, inflate round the calfs, thighs and elsewhere to restrict the gravitationally dictated arrival of blood to the lower extremities. I was not wearing a G suit because I didn't know of their existence and maybe the lads forgot; maybe!

Secondly, no one had described the actual cause of a blackout so I could hardly be expected to know how to combat this overpowering sensation.

Thirdly, a large brown paper sick bag was placed under a clip in front of me on the panel. The lamb was to the slaughter led. The ground lad strapped me in.

'Have they told you what to do?' he whispered.

'Not really,' say I. 'I'll just relax and play it cool.'

'Fatal,' says my life-saving pal, 'screw all your muscles up tight when it hits you and it's nearly the same as a G suit.'

'What's a G suit?' says I with my James Bond confidence seeping out of my feet.

'Screw yourself up, that's all,' and with that he was away. I would have given a considerable sum of money, at that point, for the cork I mentioned earlier. My celestial guide and, I hoped, saviour was the C.O. of the whole shebang, one Nobby Clark: aviator par excellence and cool as a mountain stream. The five jets took off down the runway and whooshed past the more humble of their brethren with a marked disdain.

Up in the air life suddenly turned quiet. There is no unnecessary intercom talking among these guys. Twisting my head I could see two aircraft of our right-hand formation slightly astern of my shoulder blade and not more than twelve feet away. It all became very unreal. As I think back to this once only occasion I am tempted to write of the feelings that I enjoyed. Panic, nausea, helplessness and sundry other difficult to describe feelings can be imagined if I describe the actual patterns we traced across the clear early-morning Pembrokeshire skies. There was a close-formation turn to the left and then one to the right. A full power loop-the-loop was followed by something called a barrel roll. At best my recollections are hazy because at the start of the first left-hand turn I was sure I was going to die. Apparently, Nobby checked with me before executing any manoeuvre and taking my graven image as consent we went through the card.

To pull away from the gravity of the earth at something like 600 miles an hour is so basically opposite to the human body that I was reduced to a torpor. It really was the end of the world for me. Down on the ground admiring crowds of Navy and visiting fliers watched these silver darts, seemingly glued into a perfect formation, twist and turn, disappear into the sun and reappear with ear-shattering roars, screams, claps and bangs.

It was a totally destroyed Yorkshire lad that was unstrapped as we finally rolled to a halt. Internally finished but externally the same as before take off. Many and universal were the congratulations. No blackout and an unused

90

sick bag. Little did they, or I, know the damage that had been done. First, I was unwell for two weeks, and how! Second, to this day I have never been able to fly again without experiencing abject terror.

Back, however, to the Fleet Air Arm who had by no means finished with me for, unbelievably, worse was to come. I was there officially to open the Air Day at which some 25,000 people were expected. It was arranged that I should make an appearance arriving in a small Tiger Moth plane. That was before my death-defying jet exploits. Therefore it was decreed that only the original twin-seat Hunter that I had so thankfully left was good enough to use as my fly-past aircraft. Brilliant suggestions of mine that it would look better if I arrived on a bicycle or ran at full speed down the runway were brushed aside. Diamond Six, for that was now my new name by right, would flash past in his very own jet. The temptation to sneak out of a back door and catch a train was overpowering but impossible as I was the centre of attraction.

My second appearance in the Welsh skies nearly succeeded in doing what the first one only just failed to achieve. My new pilot was an incredible all-rounder. Becoming the captain of a naval frigate before he was thirty and yearning for new fields to conquer he had taken to the skies and was now a full-strength jet-fighter pilot. Also he didn't give a bugger about anything, including the rules. And of course he just had to be as handsome as any film star, didn't he. So, with my new out of this world pal, that's almost where we started off.

He took off going straight up and the G force made me look like a road accident. Squashed and flattened to the seat like some trampled bug I felt bad upon bad.

'Have a go,' shouted this rogue Greek god.

'No thanks,' says I with deep and sincere feeling.

'Go on,' says Adonis, mistaking my refusal for politeness,

91

'these are very obedient and you can't stall 'em 'cos you can sit 'em on their arse up to 40,000 feet.'

Terrified lest he demonstrate this close of play manoeuvre I laid hold of the stick. Whereupon he promptly let go and busied himself with what looked like office work.

Have you ever flown a jet fighter? It is actually the most super fun. I flew this one in a dead straight line and had I been left alone would have continued on just such a trajectory until we plunged into the sea, out of fuel, somewhere north of Ireland. The idea of actually moving the stick left or right was totally abhorrent to me. After he had filled in his pools, or whatever it was he was about, I was immediately upbraided for not having a look at Snowdon, or Milford Haven or Cardiff. All three being about a seven minute round trip. And so we dallied in the sky, filling time in till we were due to land. Such an experience I doubt to ever have again. Incredibly and unbelievably marvellous. Also, miraculously, I was feeling on top of the world. The time in our lonesome heaven passed all too quickly and now was the hour. A last evil thought was born in my too-much pal's mind. Taking us down to sea level some considerable number of miles from land he radioed the control tower.

'We're coming in now but we'll do a flash past just under Mach one, and tell the people that Jimmy is flying the aircraft because he is as of right now.'

And so I made my most spectacular appearance ever. At just under the speed of sound, in front of now 30,000 people, with a hiss, a clap and a God-awful roar, my hands of steel on the stick and we were up up and away. And I wished I could have flown on for ever. It was the Everest of all feelings.

The Air Day was a huge success, I was a huge success, I was also well knackered and I hope my Navy flier doesn't get the sack for breaking every rule that was ever made for untrained passengers!

CHAPTER SEVEN

By now it will be obvious to the reader, as it had been obvious to me for some time, that here was indeed an unusual life, based on fun and backed up by a considerable business acumen, sufficient money and plenty of time.

One of the reasons I may have lasted so long is that I was never really fashionable so therefore I couldn't ever go out of fashion. If anything I was always one jump ahead of fashion. My initial efforts to promote disc jockeying as a living had been ten years before their time. While the Rolling Stones were still at school my hair was already shoulder length. Mick Jagger once pointed that out in an interview.

Very often I would find myself with only one pair of shoes and for several years could only boast two suits, neither of which I ever wore. My garb was a mixture of track suits, bedroom slippers and a wide assortment of T-shirts. Such a strange wardrobe was because of a marked disinclination to go shopping, a trait which many men will understand, and the fact of having no wife to be embarrassed by me looking a ragbag.

My way-out gear for Top of the Pops was motivated entirely by what was good for a laugh. A Roman legionnaire's outfit with the S.P.Q.R. standard in one hand and a mike in the other; a suit of real bananas; kaftans before they were even called kaftans; hats with lights on, and pointed shoes over a foot long. It was all great fun, provided you lived in a world of your own. The reason the B.B.C. stood for me was that if you turned the picture off you would get a normal programme presentation, for I took care not to match my chat to my dress. Nor would I ever mention what I was wearing. It was left to the public to draw their own conclusion as to what motivated me to don such odd clobber. Sometimes it worked out a longer laugh than I anticipated.

I decided to go to Moscow. For no other reason than that I had never been there before. For instance, sitting in a cinema in London, well disguised, it occurred to me that I had never been to the Isles of Scilly. Jumping up before the film had finished I rushed back to my small hotel, grabbed a few things and caught the night sleeper to Penzance. It was wintertime so a seat on the inter-island helicopter was easy and I arrived, unannounced, in that famous collection of natural beauty.

'Where to?' asked the surprised gentleman who was summoned to drive me from the heliport.

'Don't know,' says I, 'take me for a drive.'

'Can't,' says he, 'we only have nine miles of road in all the isles.'

A super four days I had amid the surprised residents. Life is good when it can be like that.

The Moscow trip was hysterical. Quite a long battle it was for me to get a visa. It was in the late 1950s and the cold war was really cold. A Britisher to go to Moscow on his own, for no reason, was definitely suspect. Eventually it was all sorted out, providing I did as I was told, and off I flew. My Russian saga started at Lime Grove TV studios where I had to do a show called Juke Box Jury. This left me with just enough time to catch the plane provided I didn't change my clothes. All this was well before colour TV and to get some impact on black and white one had to wear stark contrasts. My outfit was a light biscuit-coloured suit, gold bowtie, bright green patent shoes and a pink shirt. More sober gear was in my bag as not even I could elect to go to Moscow, at that time, in such a technicolour garb.

To change, en route, would have been easy—except they put my bag on the wrong plane. It was while changing planes at Copenhagen airport they gave me this charming information and left me with a brightly coloured exterior and a decidedly grey feeling inside. Even nowadays you should try arriving at Moscow airport at dead of night dressed like that with no baggage and no overcoat. In those strange political days it was a real stopper. To say I was an object of interest in that uniform land is to chronicle mildly. Used as I was to being looked at, it was with sinking feelings that I stepped into the life cycle of 250 million Soviet workers. From the Red Square to the incredible park of the Pavilions of Soviet Achievements and Gorky Street to Gum, the Gilbert & Sullivan of all department stores, I brought Moscow if not to a halt, at least to a much slowing of its original pace.

Two cameos will suffice for this story. One feeling and one factual. First I nearly got shot. After some days of limousine travel with a chauffeur and pretty eighteen-year-old guide— I had to hire both before I could get a visa—and having seen many buildings, official roadways and suchlike, I had demanded to see a Catholic church. I like to thank the Boss for good times and had casually asked where there was a church we might pass. After several days it dawned on me that my Russian dolly bird hadn't the slightest intention of taking me to one, or that there even was a church in Moscow.

There was indeed, so I heard, a Catholic church within the American Embassy, but I wanted an outside one. 'Find me a church,' I demanded.

'We are going to the museum,' said Olga, or Katrina or whoever she was.

'A church,' says I, thinking of the good pounds I'd paid and determined to get what I wanted.

So off we zoomed about fifteen miles to a building that looked like a derelict brick shed. Washing was drying on clothes lines in its overgrown gardens. A twenty-inch extractor fan blew from some basement work area and a ground-floor door admitted us into a strange room with no visible altar and no chairs or pews. It was some form of ecclesiastical chamber but not a church as I knew one.

'No good,' says I, getting back in the car. 'Is there a Catholic church in Moscow or isn't there?'

She either didn't know or didn't want to but under my, by now, Al Capone pressure, directed the chauffeur back into town to stop outside a large double gate of sheet iron. Well padlocked it was but through a crack I could see a fairly large building with what could be, with a willing imagination, a stone cross up on the roof. As no entry was to be gained by the big gate I walked round the wall to see if there was a side door. That was my first mistake as I was obliged not to leave my guide.

The second mistake was finding a side door and giving it a large disgruntled kick with my foot. This promptly opened and I was confronted, and terrified, by a six foot plus Russian dressed like even Hollywood wouldn't be able to manage. From black fur hat, thick double breasted greatcoat, and short black jackboots, this guy filled the gateway. Forgetting that I looked like Finian's Rainbow and gave him a much bigger turn, I coughed politely and said, 'Church Catholic?' Ivan the Terrible stood and looked at me in shock. Feeling that my pidgin English was not exactly warming the cold war I resorted to mime. Making the sign of the cross and putting my hands together as in prayer or supplication had a dramatic effect on this captain of the cossacks. Apparently he feared that it was some sort of preliminary Kung Fu attack for, with a hoarse shout, he stepped back and drew from a Sam Browne holster a hand gun—nay, cannon—with a bore on it like the exhaust of my Rolls-Royce.

Several things happened at once. Round the corner trotted my little girlfriend obviously looking for her strayed capitalist lamb. In one sweep I had her by the back of the neck

96

and, gentleman to the last, held her in front of me hoping that Ivan the Quick-Draw Terrible was at least a gentleman of honour and wouldn't shoot a lady. There ensued a two-way conversation which was terminated abruptly by the chauffeur appearing on the scene and barking about four words. Russian chauffeurs are not necessarily just drivers so it would seem. Climbing back into the car I reflected that the Good Lord was no doubt pleased with my efforts to offer thanks but I never did get to know if there is a going concern Catholic church in Moscow.

Now a feeling. Moscow was full of a strange atmosphere. Well, to me anyway. The buildings, heavy and square, gave off unusual vibes. Lenin's sarcophagus and the blank walls of the Kremlin plunged me in sombre reflective mood.

It all clicked into place the day I went to the park that houses those incredible pavilions that tell the story of the Russian regions: each building, grand in structure and different in design, standing like Disney creations on either side of an avenue as wide, straight and imposing as only Russian planners can do so well. Inside these enormous fantasies were the fruits and results of the particular region, all in museum-like display and silence. High up round the walls, great full-face pictures of stern men and women looked down to silence the visitors. All these pictures are of sons of the soil who have performed well for their masters. Except there are no masters save the state, therefore everybody is his neighbour's master, or friend, whichever your ideology.

Suddenly it all struck me. Everything was tombstones. I was in a fantastic graveyard of things past. It was a most uncanny feeling. Remember that I was alone, unable to communicate with the silent crowds about me. As it happens it was not an unpleasant feeling, sort of nice and spooky. Some years later I was in East Berlin. There is an enormous mass grave there built by the Russians. The number of entombed clients is, I think, 15,000 in three huge sunken plots, landscaped into an enormous surrounding wall where the curious can promenade. The feeling, looking down on this vast amphitheatre of death, was identical to the feeling of that bizarre park of pavilions, and Lenin's tomb.

Like caviar, such sights and feelings can become an acquired taste. It takes all sorts to make up this most unusual world.

As I always seem to have time for things, and people, it follows that my advice is much sought after by individuals and groups. Not that I like giving advice. One's own life can be quite difficult enough to manage without getting involved with others. As to my qualifications for an agony page consultant, let's just look: born weak and grown strong, ditto skint and loaded; from hard, coalface work to a perpetual crumpet-laden idleness. That I chose to fill my days and nights with hospital work and fund-raising efforts didn't alter the fact that, basically, I only had to work for money about half a day a week. From cheap holidays with wealthier relations to beautifully boring £300 a week hotel suites all over the world.

Obviously with such a life of opposites plus an unusually retentive memory, it figures that I knew quite a bit about the ups and downs of this world, and the strange habits of the people who populate it. Many, therefore, have been the young men who would seek advice as to how to get on. Of these and their development I could almost write another book. For this first attempt, suffice to say that several of them now have incomes over £500 a week, but there's a ten to one ratio of those who didn't make it.

Picked at random from these lads who are all still my friends here is a tale of one of them. Dave is his name and he developed into a sort of driver-companion. Coming from one of those, oh to be preserved, Coronation Street areas of Manchester, he was a typical product of a heavily populated big city area. Just over five feet tall and at all times clean, quiet and polite, lurking beneath this admirable exterior was a burning desire to get on. By attaching himself to my life cycle there were no weekly wages for him but a world of experience to be part of and, if he chose, to learn from.

To be a disc jockey like me was his ambition. He had been around for a couple of years without setting the world on fire and one day, after a brooding silence, demanded to know why he had not 'got on'. My strong point is descriptive analysis. 'Look,' says I (we were driving through Manchester at the time), 'if you jumped out of this car now and mingled with the crowd, no one would notice you 'cos you look just like all the other lads. Sure, smart and fashionable-looking but there's millions of guys like that. Now, if I got out, even in somewhere like Australia where I've never been, I stick out because of my distinctive appearance. People would ask "who on earth is that?" You gotta be different.'

Dave, always a silent one, withdrew into a positive abyss of constructive thought. For the rest of that day and evening he brooded.

At lunchtime the following day I answered his knock on my flat door and nearly died with shock. His hair was a violent green! A note of explanation will help. Slim, slight and dapper he was. Bald he was not, for his pride and joy was his hair. Dark, curly, luxurious, and always groomed, it covered most of him above the collar. That it should suddenly turn violent green created a most startling effect. He looked like a sort of Martian.

In silence I let him in and he made the tea. After an hour's silence I was asked for an opinion on the hairstyle. 'Great,' says I. 'If you can carry it you've cracked it.'

He wasn't quite sure what I meant by 'carry it.' What I meant was that to be different in this world requires great strength. In the animal kingdom, let a budgie fly into the open and the sparrows kill it. If you don't belong, life can get very strange, therefore Dave would have to live with this spectacular difference but, as yet, had not tasted what it was like. His baptism came at 3.0 a.m. the next morning.

He was driving me to London and we had pulled in to a motorway service area. I can never go into motorway cafés without bringing them to a grinding, autograph-laden halt. I was finally cured of trying to have a normal meal in one such place by the girl on the counter suddenly producing a large pillowcase containing at least two hundred assorted autograph books. 'Can you sign these before you go?' says she. If you don't you are definitely no good and booed out of the place. If you do sign 'em, and allowing thirty seconds for each book, that's nearly two hours. Don't doubt these figures or think that it doesn't happen because it does.

For my green-haired monster things were different as no one knew who he was. Pulling on to the transport part I sent him for a flask of tea and sandwiches. This was to be his first public appearance. At 3.0 a.m. in a transport café life is low-key. Conversations are quiet and lone drivers nod over cooling teas. Dave's path from the door to the counter caused mixed reactions. One knight of the road with an involuntary muscular action sent a mouthful of tea up his nose instead of down his gullet and the surprised fluid cascaded down his nostrils back into his mug. All conversations drained away to a silence.

The worst was yet to come. The young lady who served things would turn the scale at perhaps thirteen cheerful stone. She also came from one of the West Indian islands. Such happy and cheerful souls are noted for loud and lively laughter. I bear witness to the fact that, when startled, they can scream with incredible gusto. Dave had approached the counter in an accumulated silence. This had caused several nodding drivers to nod off. The Jamaican lady was also having forty winks, but stood up against the warm tea boiler. Upon opening her eyes and seeing my small green-haired

Dave scowling at her, she gave a piercing scream. Several sleepy drivers had near heart attacks. Others who had not noticed Dave's arrival in their midst uttered hoarse cries. The lady, moved with fear to her ancestral soul, gave another trumpet of terror. Dave's request for a flask of tea and two sandwiches fell on deaf ears. By this time it was apparent, even to him, that his life had changed dramatically, also that he was not going to get served. Having seen the whole performance through the windows, I collapsed with laughter. Dave returned to the car in a towering rage. He was furious and called for terrible things to happen to the serving lady, her next of kin, all lorry drivers and anyone who didn't have green hair.

For six months he sported his terrifying banner and for me life was a laugh a minute. For Dave was torn between the desire to 'get on' and a total non-comprehension of why people laughed, or leapt, when he was around but lorded me, with my blond mop. Without a doubt the funniest scene I was not witness to, but got the confirmati n and an incredible sequel almost a year later. It was like this.

At that time I was living in a small hotel in Bloomsbury. Nearby were some parking meters that gave you ten hours for five old sixpences, half a crown. Arriving, on this particular occasion, at 3.0 a.m. it was necessary for Dave to sleep in the caravan so he could wake up and feed the meter at 8.0 a.m. As it happens, he overslept and at about 10 a.m. along came the law to tow it, or drive it, away. One officer was left to this task whilst his colleague went off to look for other clients. To start my van was a work of art as it was a diesel engine which needed pre-heating before it would fire. Sitting in the seat, to get in had been easy for the copper, but trying to find the starter was a puzzling task. In the back of the van, Dave of the green hair had been awakened by his movements and sounds. Thinking it was me and realizing he had overslept, he threw open the connecting door.

Several things happened at once. The officer, startled at the sliding door noise of what he had presumed to be an empty vehicle, screwed round in his seat. Dave sleeps in the nude. Confronted by a naked dwarf with a tousled mop of green hair proved too much for the guardian of the law. With a cry of alarm he abandoned ship. Dave, thinking the lawman was a thief, rushed forward to do battle but the lawman had gone. All of this was duly recounted to me later and it provided me with a good laugh.

About a year later I happened to be talking to a policeman outside the hotel. Discussing this and that, I mentioned the long past incident. It had an electrifying effect on the copper. 'You're not kidding Jim, are you?' said he.

'Course not,' says I.

'Strewth,' says the copper. 'When matey got back to the station and tried to tell us that a naked green-haired midget had suddenly appeared from nowhere we really thought he'd gone round the bend. I've got to go back and straighten it out.'

And off he went to clear the name of the innocent but for so long disbelieved policeman.

CHAPTER EIGHT

It was obvious that my wild leaping about all over the country contained perfect ingredients for a radio show. The Beeb took me out for lunch, asked me if I'd like to work for them, and, hey presto, Savile's Travels was born. At the time of this writing it's been running seven years and is the longest running, unchanged show on Radio One. Five years ago another top show was added to my list of long runners, Speakeasy. Part of the religious department of the B.B.C., this great talk show attracted government ministers, top churchmen and all manner of celebrities who know that to be on Speakeasy will give them a perfect showcase for their particular scene. Possibly the most listened-to talk show on any of the radio networks, it catapulted me right up into the brain market. Very good for the ego but it could be bad for business. Let me explain.

There are literally tens of thousands of brainy people and even though it was nice to be thought of as clever, there was only one Jimmy Savile and he was doing quite well, thank you, without having to mix it with intellectuals. Speakeasy has run now for five years but I watch it with a wary eye and hang on grimly to Savile's Travels, a good fun show, and Top of the Pops, the TV show that really put me, and kept me, at the top. I've always said that brains can be a handicap and keep insisting that I don't have many, but will admit to plenty of animal cunning!

It was probably my animal streak and rebelling against my rich cosy world that caused me to set off on what was to be, without doubt, the toughest physical assignment to date: to walk the distance from John o' Groat's to Land's End. A formidable feat for anyone, but for a rich man who can live good and easy it was a nutter thing to do. Considerable planning was necessary as my radio shows had to be done and I had exactly thirty-one days in between appearances on Top of the Pops. The Beeb were magnificent and fixed four separate broadcasts of Speakeasy at various points from north to south. The Nationwide news programme arranged to do progress film reports. Leeds Infirmary arranged for my ever faithful friend Charles to find me from time to time and check I wasn't going round the bend. Northern Dairies sent an executive friend, Peter, to keep up with supplies of good foods. Broadmoor Hospital loaned my good friend Don to drive behind in the support caravan and he was relieved by Perce, the law lord of the Manchester cab ranks, and brother Vince who had just come out of the Navy after thirty-six years. All in all it was a major operation.

Why on earth I should want to walk from John o' Groat's to Land's End I have no idea. Except I wanted to and I did. March was the month I chose and for good reason. The pain difference between March winds and snow and, say, June's basking breezes is not much. It hurts just as much in June. The difference is that in March people say, 'How can you do it in such terrible conditions?' whereas in May people say, 'It must have been a nice summer's walk.'

My departure from John o' Groat's was a pantomime. About 4,000 wellwishers turned up to wish me bon voyage, nearly an all-time record for the hamlet. A piercing wind and freezing temperature caused all 4,000 to try and cram into the local hotel where my considerable team were now lunching, packed like oats into a haggis. The temperature shot up inside and turned it into a sauna. There were several faintings and a claustrophobic hysteric, during which time I was standing on a chair, signing autographs and being fork fed by a local lovely as it was impossible to work knife, fork and pen. Out into the icy wind and the entire multitude set off in high spirits. After three miles and having sorted out wife to husband, children to parents and an assortment of excited animals to owners, the road stretched long and grim, before my hunched body and narrowed eyes: because it had to be a gale force headwind, didn't it.

The four weeks of self-imposed toil that followed ranks as the most painful, dedicated, and beautiful period of an already overcrowded life. Painful because no training can toughen normal feet and legs to sustain nearly 1,000 miles (actually, 937 as it worked out). Dedicated because the temptation to stop, get on a bus, throw yourself under one, or refuse to get out of bed in a morning, is overpowering and only a cast-iron determination can make one go on. Beautiful because that's what it was. The treeless wild that is Caithness. Walking up the Pass of Glencoe in full moon. The owl diving for its supper in the dusk. The baby rabbit that hops up to you in the night in total innocent friendship. The whole length and breadth of the country of Britain and finally the sound of the waves outside my hotel window in Penzance, knowing that there's only nine miles left to the end of the land. It was beauty of a vast, national aspect. And the people, the characters one meets and the scrapes one gets into.

My first terror was being set on by three Dobermann dogs on only the second day, but saved by my heavy plastic overgear. The dogs were shouted off my back by the farmer who admitted they were 'a wee bitty fierce, Jimmy.' Or the mad dog near Bristol that bit me, a horse, the back wheel of a mini, a passing child, and my long-suffering friend Peter who, as the fangs of the beast pierced his calf, cleared a café table like a Grand National Champion. 'It's not bad tempered,' explained its owner, 'it can't stand the colour blue.' What on earth the colour blue had to do with such a wide variety of victims I'll never know.

For laughs there was the lady in Scotland who was so intent on copping for an autograph she jumped out of her mini van and forgot to put the handbrake on. Parked on a slope, the van followed her and, much to the lady's surprise, overtook her. Running alongside the runaway vehicle the lady shouted at it to 'Stop, stop.' It cleared the village square like a rogue elephant and finally buried itself into the flank of an articulated lorry whose driver had only just paused to survey the wild scenes my striding through the townlet had caused. 'Never mind,' puffed the lady as she caught me up, 'it was only an old thing.'

To be honest, the stories of my marathon trek would fill a book on its own and I have to press on or I'll never finish this one. Before we leave this long walk saga I will try to capture the atmosphere of the night before the last day. The hotel I walked into in Penzance was a nice, quiet and gentle place. My visit all but destroyed it. Imagine such a well bred, peaceful hotel, yawning in the evening spring sunshine. The swing door opens and an exhausted, emaciated blond-haired man walks in, looks round with an experienced eye and plonks down in the largest easy chair in the foyer. That was me of course and I was well bushed. Half the population of Cornwall followed me in. In a twinkling the place was bedlam. Royal Marine Captain Chris Goode commandeered the only public phone and was shouting map references down a bad line to two helicopter pilots who were to fly above me on the morrow. The Mayor arrived unannounced and had to sit on the arm of my chair. Two priests arrived to exhort me to visit their youth club. As there were no chairs left the clerics knelt on the floor by my seat. Several reporters were milling about with pencils, pads, and cameras. To be heard one had to shout. Everybody shouted. It was total chaos and lasted for hours. As always, night works its soporific effect on all and the gang crept off to sleep, somewhere. The only casualties of the evening had been the Marine Captain and his sergeant, Neil Fisher, who had both fallen out of a window and didn't reappear till dawn.

The final scene of the night was played by two: me and the night porter. It could have cost him his life, but it didn't. It was like this.

The madness that had reigned throughout the evening had died down. The crowds had left the front of the hotel and my friends and followers had either fainted or fled. Miraculously I was alone up in my room. For a while I sat by the open window and just listened to the sea rolling about on the beach. My mind flew back up the road to the sea at John o' Groat's and it was a moving moment of the incredible month I had just undergone. Only one more day and only nine miles to cover. A stupendous feeling. Naturally I had to be well groomed for the last lap, so having borrowed shampoo and hairdryer from the housekeeper it was all down to a touch of the barnet wash and I would be nice and sparkling for the new track suit and the big finish on the morrow.

After a quick washbasin job I set about to unravel the intricacies of the portable hairdryer. It was one of those models that's slung on the shoulder like a bag. A plastic cap fits over the hair and a large-diameter pipe runs from the top of the cap to the hot-air works which, as I've said, hangs from the shoulder on a broad strap. This allows the dryer a modicum of movement; the distance of travel is dictated by the length of cable from the blower to the electric wall plug. Except that there was no electric wall plug in my room. Logical deduction was necessary. Hotels must have vacuum cleaners which must need wall plugs so where was one? The nearest socket was out in the hall. Also in the hall was a large ornamental chair like a throne. Quietly moving the enormous wooden seat a few yards meant I could sit, like King Solomon, in the silent, sleeping hall wearing the portable hairdryer. It must have been an arresting scene, me sitting there with a great tube coming from the top of my head. Especially as it didn't look like me, with all my hair pushed

107

up into the large plastic cap. Another factor not taken into account was that the hairdryer emitted a high-pitched whine.

Three floors below, the night porter, shattered by the events of the evening, pricked up his ears at this unusual, untraceable sound. Grabbing a large torch he padded round like James Bond looking for the mystery noise. For several minutes he drew a blank, then realized it was coming from upstairs. My chair was exactly opposite the top of the stairs, which were all in darkness as it was now 4 a.m. His puffed arrival opposite me triggered off several things at the same time. First of all, he didn't see me as he was playing the torch from side to side. Secondly, as his torchlight illuminated me, the throne, and the tube coming from the top of my head, I had meant to offer him a whispered explanation. This was complicated by my cigar falling out of my mouth on to my bare legs. Instead of a whispered explanation he got a loud cry of anguish and I leaped into the air. My considerable cry was echoed by his more considerable cry of terror and the torch flew from his grasp. At the same time he shot in the air and his cry again rent the night as he fell backwards down the stairs. Fearing for his safety I grabbed the torch and hastened to his aid.

At this point we would do well to analyse his cumulative anxieties. He is first of all moved to understandable terror at coming upon a creature from another world, for no earthling would have a large tube sprouting from the top of his head. The creature is obviously up to no good sitting in a darkened corridor at 4.0 a.m. His terror is confirmed by whatever the hell it is suddenly rearing up at his approach and giving off a large shout.

His efforts to depart the scene are commendable but complicated in that he is standing on the top step of a flight going down. That he should suddenly fall arse over tit adds fright to terror. The final ingredient towards a cardiac arrest comes when I tread on his bunch of keys which he has dropped. After nine hundred miles of hard road my feet are in constant pain so a bunch of keys under my bare left sole is all I need. 'Ooh, SHITE!' I yell, and drop the torch on his head.

The arrival of roused residents adds to the mêlée. The first one peers down the steps with the classic query, 'What's going on?' The second trips over the hairdryer and butts the first arrival in the back. Mr What's Going On takes off like a seagull and lands in our midst. The start of this midnight matinée, the porter, heartened by the arrival of reinforcements, rises from the carpet and calls upon us all to search for his original creature. He is dismissed as one suffering from some delusion and to this day, like the policeman and my green-haired Dave, is never believed. I am wounded in the foot, damp on the head, and totally exhausted, so I slide off and leave them all to it.

The final day to Land's End is a tour de force which I will leave to the imagination. A sunny day, it is 31 March, exactly a month after the start. 937 miles and 20,000 autographs have gone by. Helicopters chatter above, flower-pickers rush from the fields with bunches of spring daffodils for me. Laughing and talking crowds walk along with me and suddenly, Boom, boom, boom, the band of the Royal Marines swing in alongside playing 'Congratulations'. We all walk to my personal Shangri La, Land's End. The sea twinkles, my eyes are filled with tears for the final yards. It is all over. Thank you God for such moments of happiness on earth.

CHAPTER NINE

From such heights of physical achievements I could almost finish off my life story here. Like the waves on the shore my days come and go, all filled with a fullness that is too much. I shall tell you stories from now till the end of the book. All of them true and all of them from the heart, as I use no notes for any of these writings.

Let me tell you about my O.B.E. I realize that there are many people who have received these and even greater rewards and recognitions. Also I am the first to realize that I come well, well down on God's personal honours list and there are many people without medals up to whose shoulders I will never reach even if I live to be a thousand. Be that as it may, my O.B.E. is a source of deep comfort to me if only for one reason. Imagine being able to take your mother to Buckingham Palace for a lifelong recognition.

It all started like this. Returning to my Leeds home in the early hours of one weekend morning after my usual country-wide wanderings, I was smoking a last cigar and idly sorting through some odd mail. A long envelope marked 'From the Prime Minister' caught my eye. 'What on earth can he be writing to me about' was my first reaction. It was nowhere near election time so he couldn't be wanting to borrow my many million audience. A second envelope was inside the first. The mystery deepened. A sort of legal type letter was inside and at first I couldn't make head nor tale of it. It appears I was 'most excellent' and that I was an 'ordinary officer' or something. At two o'clock in the morning it was not easy to deduce so I took it paragraph by paragraph. Halfway through I nearly died with fright. I was going to be crowned, or knighted or some such. I swear before God that my first reaction was to grab the envelope and check the name and address, for I was convinced I was reading something meant for another and such realization gives an immediate feeling of guilt. It dawned on me that this was, as they say, IT! The sensation which follows the realization is akin to a sudden skid in a car or being disturbed by some girl's father.

In times of stress or surprise one acts strangely. I folded the letter, put it back in the two envelopes and sat down. Then started from the beginning all over again. Indeed I was being asked if I would accept an O.B.E. if offered one. Would I, oh boy; I could just see the Duchess's face. It would register a mild disapproval at first as she always had a lurking suspicion that I would come unstuck, sooner or later. Then she would get on with her knitting. The letter warned me to say nowt to nobody. Were I to breathe a word the whole deal would be null and void. It was too big to keep and somebody had to share it, but who to ring at, now, 2.30 a.m.?

My brother Vince, in Cardiff, was the victim. Asleep he was, and took the telephoned news with all the excitement of a chief petty officer R.N. who has just been awakened. Which was nil. Well, almost nil as he did grunt something about 'very good, very good' before he rang off. Sleep for me was out of the question so I turned to my ever awake, friendly building, Leeds Infirmary. Walking unconcernedly into the casualty department I was looking for tea and company. Having shared the news with Vince I could now keep quiet.

Within minutes of getting into the hospital there came a job to move a dead body from a ward to the mortuary. 'I'll do it,' says I, and set off with a colleague porter. Wheeling the remains of the departed soul through half-lit corridors brought everything back to perspective. What cared she, for it was a lovely old lady, for my excitement? Her race had been run and she was now where it really mattered, in heaven. Refreshed and restored, I went back home and slept like a log.

The announcing of the honours list meant many headlines for me, and congratulations poured in from all over the world. At this point let me just dwell on this award-getting business. Embarrassment, guilt, pride and a mild form of agoraphobia are the first feelings. Embarrassment because we are really all equal but we happen to live in an odd society structure. Guilt because we know of many who deserve more than us. Pride, in its mildest sense, because most of human achievements are a little prideful, and a mild form of agoraphobia because all who know you, and in my case it was millions, have something to say about it so *that* takes you back to the start, of being slightly embarrassed.

There is an old military saying, 'Win 'em and wear 'em,' so that had to be my decision. Where my name went so my award went. Posters and press carry it on my instruction and that's that. I am in an exuberant business so I might as well be honest and unashamed at the same time.

Our palace day was a circus, a riot and a bull's eye all in one. I say 'our palace day' for that's what it was. My honour had been given for, mainly, my voluntary hospital work. As I had worked for seven years with the same porter, Joe, he came too. Then the Duchess. Then, to drive, my pal Don from Broadmoor hospital. Sundry other friends joined the gang including a pal from Scotland Yard who joined us in the Savile's Travels caravan by running at ten m.p.h. across the square in front of the palace and hurling himself aboard before we hit the gates. Guests on these occasions are strictly limited to two and no more. With no disrespect to royal decree there were eleven of us inside my vehicle and it was easier for the gate to let us in than try to sort us out. A word first about my official team, the Duchess and Joe.

The Duchess was totally disbelieving of the whole thing.

112

It was just the latest in a long, bewildering series of unlikely events. She fortified herself against unknown disaster by bringing both her knitting and crocheting. As for Joe, a true and real saint of a human being, it was an emotional experience rather like the morning after winning the pools. My Joe is a superman in the non-muscular sense: slight of build, ever smiling and totally honest and sincere as only a man modest in money can be. Modest in money he may be but a millionaire in human terms, the like of which I could never be. Joe will talk to anybody, and did. Startled regal figures of medal-gaining moment were all embraced by Joe's universal greeting of the occasion. 'There's never been a day like this' and 'There'll never be another day like this' were his two confidential, buttonholing expressions. Joe thought they had all come to see me, him, and the Duchess.

The ceremony in the throne room was of the order of magnificence that only 1,000 years of tradition can sustain. The Queen Mum was the disher-out on this occasion and my conversation, private as befitting decency, went on for a lot longer than normally allocated. Afterwards, the boss of Decca records, Sir Edward Lewis, for whom I had worked so long on Radio Luxembourg, gave a celebration lunch. By now the Duchess had assumed an angle of 45°, from the realization that it was all true, and Joe, normally slightly stooped, was almost bent double. Even for me it was a bit of a physical marathon.

Evening saw my shattered twosome back on the train north and for me it happened to coincide with one of my rare dance hall appearances, at the Top Rank in Croydon. In full morning dress and glittering medal I weaved the spell over 2,000 teen-types and at 1.0 a.m. couldn't find the strength to make it across London so I walked into an adjacent hotel and slept for twelve hours.

It was not long after this peak of life's happenings that the Duchess decided to die. I was three hundred miles away from her at the time. She was eighty-five, had just had a good night out at bingo, climbed into bed, and called it a day. She was staying with my sister Chris, which was a blessing. It was 2.30 a.m. before I was tracked down to Bournemouth, in the very seafront flat I had acquired for her to spend her remaining winters. She never ever saw it. It was nearly bedtime for me and I was just having a final smoke when I got the news. 'Thank you,' said I to the friend who'd found me, 'leave it with me', and put the phone down. I sat there for an hour, feeling a small ache turn into a big one. When you've lived all your life with someone and they leave you to go it alone, it's a very strange feeling. There was much to be done and as I fixed things for the final personal appearance of the Duchess it gave me the exact feeling that I was actually fixing to bury my own body. In some ways, I was.

Her funeral snowballed into an incredible day. It is easy to organize a wedding but difficult to organize a funeral. It's easy to fix the time, place and suchlike but one doesn't send invitations to funerals so how do you know how many friends are coming to pay their respects? So I organized for the immediate family and left the rest wide open. The morning of her last day above this earth, traffic wardens appeared and masked off all meters in the streets surrounding St Anne's Cathedral in Leeds. A dozen policemen led by an inspector appeared to handle things with quiet dignity. All the Sunday honorary staff of the cathedral turned up to officiate inside. Even a taxi rank was organized outside, and all of this without me raising a finger.

What sort of memorial turn-out do you get for a lady that at seventy was practically unknown, but at eighty-five was a superstar? The answer is, over 2,000. Three times as many as for midnight mass at the cathedral at Christmas. From all walks of life they came. From governments, official bodies, political parties. From hospitals, homes and foreign countries. And think not it was because of me, dear friend, for

114

I knew but a handful. These were the people the Duchess had met and captured with her innocent magic, and they came to see her, not me. That I know for sure. Her charisma went even beyond personal friends. The entire night-duty staff of the Leeds ambulance service stayed out of bed, went up to the cemetery, and formed a guard of honour to escort her from the gates to the grave. And she had never met any one of them. If you think they all of them turned up because of me I'll have a small bet with you. If I die while I'm famous fifty million people may notice it on the TV and in the press but I doubt if 500 will come to say goodbye. A mother is far more of a pull than a son and that's the way it should be.

Strange things happened during that twenty-four hours. Here's two. As I have said, the Duchess died in the arms of my sister Chris. It fell to Chris's lot to take charge of her personal effects. One of these was her wedding ring. At the time of my equally loved father's death, the Duchess had given me his wedding ring and I ever since wore it on the third finger of my right hand. It follows, therefore, that I would give the earth to have my mother's wedding ring for my little finger. A sentimental duo quite priceless to me. We are a very equal family and no one of us commands the other so Chris had the Duchess's wedding ring by right, and that was that. 'You can have from me what you want for the ring,' says I to Chris. 'One day, perhaps,' says Chris, 'but not just yet.' And quite right too.

The Duchess, up in heaven, was not necessarily in agreement with this loose arrangement. I had always wanted she should die with me but I'd obviously lost out on that one, but her wedding ring was even then destined to rest on my hand, alongside that of her much loved husband. The day before the funeral was a Sunday. We had moved the Duchess from the east coast to my sister Joan's house in Leeds. I had been doing a job for the local Little Sisters of the Poor and was hurrying back to Joan's. Chris was snoozing in a chair when she suddenly sprang awake and started pulling at her finger. Joan, startled, shot up and said, 'What's wrong?' 'Mother's ring,' cried Chris, 'it's burning my finger.' Sure enough, her finger, with our mother's wedding ring on, had turned red and swollen and all in a matter of minutes. The two girls rushed to the tap and with Chris in high distress managed to pull the ring off. At that moment I walked in the front door. 'Here,' said Chris, giving me that which I had so much wanted, 'Mother wants you to have this.' Both girls and several witnesses corroborate this story.

Equally true, but in lighter vein, was this happening. My brother Vince was nearly always in the Duchess's black books for not writing to her more often. As a family we are not regular letter-writers at the best of times but the Duch always had this fixation about Vince. It had turned into a family joke. Up from Cardiff came Vince, and he was to receive a last telling off from the greatest mother of all time. Brothers John and Vince, together with brothers-in-law Arthur and Jack (both the latter staunch devotees of the Duchess), carried her to the high altar of the church. Seeking places in the front pew, the only one I'd reserved for the family, there was room left for all—except Vince. So he had to sit elsewhere. Up at the cemetery, once again he got the maternal elbow for, by the time he'd got himself ready to leave for the tea and buns, all the cars had gone and he had to go out to the road and hitch a lift for the three miles back into town! This was a great laugh, in the nicest sense, for him and all of us because the Duchess could be as subtle as the Godfather when she chose to be.

Apart from the pain of losing my only real love in this world I have a great peace, comfort and thankfulness to God since she died. It works out like this. She had a great life and a great death. Her final minutes saw her with her family, a priest, and, for good measure, a doctor. There was no pain and no lingering. She was blessed by God to go so peacefully.

Therefore I am eternally thankful. Plus when she was alive I had to share her with the world. Now I feel she's all mine. And that's the way it is.

So for me, life gets funnier, stranger, faster, fitter, more flash and just more than ever before. It should be all very exhausting but it's not really. People tell me they wouldn't like to be in my shoes. By this I am mystified but grateful as my present shoes are a sight more comfortable than my pit boots.

Things happen to me that don't really happen to normal people. A friend of mine in the south of England died and I went along to his cremation. On such occasions I really try to be inconspicuous but I am very difficult to disguise. Sure enough, creeping in behind a handful of unaware mourners I am spotted by an eagle-eyed gardener. A tap on the shoulder and I am invited, by nods and motions, behind the scenes to the business half of the crematorium. Politely showing an interest in the somewhat gruesome impedimenta I am offered the well meant but astounding job of frying my own pal. This I do, guided by the experts, and rake out his ashes an hour and twenty minutes and several cups of tea later.

Things like this just don't happen to anybody else I know. Cab drivers, London ones in particular, will at least once a week carry me somewhere then refuse to take any money. This is entirely opposite to their newspaper image but at least I know them for what they do on their charity outings and know that there are far, far more good cab drivers than sharks.

I was once asked, quite illegally, if I would like to drive a full-size, main-line passenger train, and the driver, lulled by my obvious instant expertise, fell fast asleep in the other seat. Actually there's not a lot of difference between a diesel engine and my tram car escapade of a previous chapter. Ferry boats I have steered across treacherous rivers and estuaries, and I once worked the overhead radio frequency dials in a Viscount airliner during a tricky landing at a mist-shrouded airport.

To emphasize the wide variety of my happenings a husband once said he admired the work I did so much, would I like to make love to his wife of less than a year? This I declined, but at the other end of the spectrum, at a hospital I had just called in at, I was asked by the short-staffed head porter if I could lay out the remains of an old man who had just been burned to death and his next of kin were coming within the next hour. This job I accepted because after all these years in the hospital world I am now quite good at that sort of thing.

My voluminous charity work now takes up about ninety per cent of my working and even waking time. This is not because I am any more charity-minded than anyone else. It's just that, like work, it's a fun thing and gives me some great times and laughs. It also makes vast quantities of money for other people. As for my own wages I work on the principle that the less you are seen the more they want you. This creates a seller's market so that I can charge what I want for when I want. For radio and television I can easily get anything from £150 to £500 an hour. TV commercials can bring me big lumps when I want a big lump. A typical commercial takes me half a day to film for which I can get from £10–20,000. Even more if I really want it.

After the novelty of having lots of money wears off, it becomes relatively unimportant. Therefore, having reasonably provided for my old age means lots of money-earning capacity but not so much need, so what better than to give it away. The biblical saying, 'those who give shall receive' is very true. In my case anyway, because the more I make for all sorts of charities, most definitely the more health and happiness I get from the Good Lord.

What I am doing here is making clear to all how I have finished up as a one-man charity band. I prefer to operate alone as a catalyst which goes in, creates, and gets out. Example. Five years of the Jimmy Savile walk in Dublin has made the kids' clinic there over £50,000. My annual appearance attracts an average of 30,000 sponsored walkers for that day. A Christmas letter for an old folks' organisation nets over £12,000. Half a dozen TV appeals for all sorts of charities brings in nearly £100,000. These are just odd ones picked out at random from my mind, but over ten years, and still going strong, I've made well over a million pounds.

Just for the record, from all this money I take not even expenses. One has to be terribly careful when dealing with the charity world. Some years ago I took a wages job, for me, from an agent. A huge crowd turned up at Alfreton in Derbyshire, and after the hullabuloo I found out it was one of those functions where any profit went to local charities. My modest fee in those days was £150. I was paid direct by the London agent and, sure enough, some months later a lady wrote to me asking for my fee for the charity. I wrote back and said she could certainly have what the income tax had left me out of the original. It taught me a great lesson: to check all jobs out first. Working now as a catalyst means that all I do is just turn up and let all the local committees handle all money things. People still say that my charity work is well publicized. Of course it is, because if I wasn't advertised as being there in the first place no one would turn up and there'd be no profit. The obvious answer to unkind people is that I had quite enough money to retire to the South of France before I ever started this never-ending round of free appearances.

Let me tell you about the fun part of the charity deal. I got a call one day from the chairman of a local council. He'd got a new idea for the annual mayoral ball and wanted to turn it into a big youth dance, and would I come? For years the affair had been just a bit stuffy and only attracted a couple of hundred locals. He wanted 2,000 and did I have any ideas? Sure I had. Good ideas are my strong point. I will come, to Otley in Yorkshire it was, if you will arrange for me to sleep in a tent up the local hillside with another tent alongside with six girls to sleep there as my bodyguards!

My demands really put the dance on the map and 2,000 tickets went like hot cakes. My ultimatum of 'no tents, no girls, no me' meant the council had to go through with it.

A notice for volunteers in the paper brought well over a hundred young lady applicants, all determined to spend a night on the moors. The council had to decide which six, so they called a special meeting. Some of the members only then realized what they were doing. 'We can't have a council meeting to decide which six of our girls sleep with this man,' said several, more bewildered than outraged. So half the council left and half stayed. Six girls were selected and all of them were given matching mini skirts and white boots, as befitting a ceremonial bodyguard. They looked good enough to eat. I duly arrived in the town and it was the start of an incredible evening. The first thing was that the father of one of the girls arrived and hauled her off home. She protested loudly but dad would have none of this preposterous situation. For company I had brought along a millionaire pal who just didn't believe my story. When he saw the crumpet his eyes shot out a mile and his total conversation for the evening was an incredulous 'Are we kipping with them?'

Technically no, as we were in the tent next door. Or were supposed to be. The dance finished in spectacular, never-before and certainly never-since fashion, and the moment of truth was upon us. What follows must be the greatest ever. It was raining but who cared. The tents had been erected in the afternoon in a secret glade known only to the chairman. The blankets and suchlike were kept in his house to avoid damp or theft. At 3.0 a.m. an unbelievable sight appeared in the sleeping town. Several cars, headed by the mayoral one, drove to the foot of the hill, a local beauty spot known as the Chevin. From the cars out climb a dozen people: five girls, me and my pal, the chairman, his wife and his equerry. On our heads we carry our blankets, and in single file, like Sherpa porters, we set off up to the tents. I was convulsed with laughter and with a real pain.

My pal, another Jimmy, was convinced he had gone mad and kept appealing to me to tell him that all this wasn't really happening. The girls had changed into anoraks and trousers, and on reaching the tents set about preparing for what was left of the night. The chairman, his lady, and minder, bade us good night and left. It was all too much and we all fell about and over each other, making enough noise to wake the dead. Needless to say the girls' tent fell over and we all had to finish up together. Dawn came and with it the council chairman and his cars. It was seven totally exhausted campers that fell back down the hill to a breakfast we couldn't eat because we had all laughed too much. There hangs on my wall in Leeds a picture with which I was presented and the inscription gives the details of our great night. So who says charity isn't fun?

Actually there is a sequel story to that one. The Yorkshire town of Bingley lies about fifteen miles from Otley. The city fathers, dazzled by Otley's civic ball escalation from 200 to 2,000, asked me if I would consider a similar escapade. Always ready for a good fun scene I came up with the following. They would build me a tree house in their beauty spot, Shipley Glen. Up in this I would kip plus, as usual, my wages of fun bodyguards—six local girls. Actually it was the mixture as before except up a tree instead of in a tent. Inquiries among the local youth organization elicited the fact that tree-builders were plentiful. Materials were available and a local farmer gladly donated temporary use of a stout secluded tree. So it was all systems go. Except that it didn't work out like I'd planned.

The tickets for the ball were a sell-out and six volunteer

young ladies were beautifully turned out in matching outfits. Once again my long-suffering pal Jimmy was hauled from counting his gold, to join this crazy escapade. The first unforeseen complication to arise was foot and mouth disease. This put the block on movements of field-dwelling beasts, into which category, apparently, fell disc jockeys, tree-house builders and anticipating dolly birds. Our field and tree were suddenly out of bounds.

Given the news with only four days to go caused me a great feeling of thwart. I also detected a note of relief in the voice of the official who telephoned me.

'All the tickets are sold, Jimmy, so why not just come and stay in a hotel?'

'Out of the question,' said I, and so it was.

All my showbiz life I've been very strict on truth. I weigh up form very carefully before I announce a stunt and then I've just got to go through with it. Once the public doesn't believe what you say, you're finished. Well, I would be anyway. Plus I could never live in peace with myself.

Foot and mouth disease is nobody's fault so a new and novel idea had to be forthcoming. It didn't take long. 'Use the tree-house material to build a raft, float it on to the river with a long rope, and we'll sleep in midstream.'

Now, dear friend, water is one element with which I am not in love. A non-swimmer, by choice plus an aversion to cold water at any time, makes a madness of the raft idea. But not really because my knowledge of the Yorkshire Dales reminded me that the River Aire at that point is only about four feet deep. Or it would have been had it not been for a cloudburst a few hours before our arrival. Another factor was that my shepherd-like knowledge of the Dales was not exactly up to ordnance-survey standard therefore I had no knowledge of a weir across the river which effectively caused the depth to rise, or worse, sink to twenty feet. The evening's prospects became laced with terror. None of this I knew as

I had been my usual gypsy self and out of contact for the preceding three days.

In my innocence and absence the stout-hearted council members and youth organizations had solemnly launched on to the boiling waters a hurriedly erected wooden platform, hopefully capable of supporting eight souls for eight hours. It didn't last eight seconds. The hungry flood water seized it and carried it off, smashing it to bits on the weir. The many cubic yards of assorted planks and logs carried on merrily out of sight and completely fouled up the Shipley waterworks some six miles downstream.

And so I arrived in the town with my pal. Pitch dark it was, blowing a gale and pouring with rain. We had picked up an official on the outskirts and as we headed for the dance he diffidently suggested that we might like to stop on the bridge and view our home for the night. Full of glee we braced over the parapet. My heart stopped. Instead of your friendly neighbourhood four-foot stream, a football-field-sized are of inky black water heaved and swelled beneath us. There is something evil about inky black water and more so when it heaves. The official produced a powerful torch and shone it down on the depths. Right in the middle of the vortex and snatching to get free was without a doubt the craziest and most lethal kip I shall ever see. A second-hand, much patched, microscopic, ex-R.A.F. survival kit, rubber raft. One of those with the inflated outer ring and rubber sheet bottom. But more, for on to this ancient wartime survivor had been erected probably the first boy-scout type tent that was ever made. The whole thing was quite unbelievable and from our vantage point looked about two inches wide.

'Tell me the story,' said I, feeling suddenly very unwell.

'That was all we could manage after the raft disintegrated,' said the hapless official.

So we went to the dance and had a great time. There were speeches and tea and sandwiches. My bodyguard girls flitted about and there was, overall, the acceptance that all my good ideas had been thwarted but never mind. It would take more than a cloudburst, twenty feet of evil water and a leaky life-raft to beat me.

'Right,' I announced at midnight like a hairy Cinderella, 'assemble the guard of honour to escort me and James to our floating bed.'

Had I announced the emigration of the entire Yorkshire cricket team it could not have caused more consternation. Consternation from all except one old and venerable gentle-man who called, in a high voice, 'There, I told you he'd go through with it.'

And so we set off for the river—the girls, the officials, several sturdy youths to reclaim the raft from midstream, and the old gent, who insisted on holding onto my arm. This nearly proved his final act because as I stepped aboard with a great flourish I fell through the bottom of the damn thing. The old gent, who was still fastened to my arm, uttered a bleat of terror as he was jerked towards the oggin. His life was saved insofar as he was fastened to friend James who, in turn, was linked onto the six girls.

A lively scene ensued. I had disappeared into the depths because one doesn't step into a rubber life-raft. One should fall in bodily so that the floor takes the even weight. As I had stepped into it with one foot the sides of the life-raft swallowed me up like some great flesh-eating water lily. Hauled ashore with my heart between my tonsils, and amid much advice and simulation, James and I were eventually laid aboard, side by side, like two corpses about to be floated off on some sacred river rite. As usual in times of stress I started to laugh. That triggered Jimmy off and as we floated off from the bank we were both in stitches. I mean, it was just too much. I really should have been certified.

For all its ridiculousness the dangers were very real. The river was well in flood and the waters roared over the weir.

124

We were held by a thirty foot rope but, fully clothed plus expensive overcoats, we would have sunk like stones. Jammed side by side, any change of position caused a great heaving and gurgling from our frail craft. Before you condemn me as totally mad, dear reader, think not that foolish honour had hastened us into this nightmare situation. For me, as with many, when danger turns up, honour is over the horizon like a whippet. It had been my foul plot to wait until the watchers on the shore had taken to their beds. Once alone, a few pulls on the lifeline and we would have been ashore, safe and warm in Jimmy's new Mercedes car. Before sunrise we would have been back in the raft ready to be hauled ashore by the youth organizations and basking in totally undeserved admiration. This is why Jimmy and I had laughed, fit to burst, as we had floated off. But if I was determined to be dishonourable, fate had quite different plans.

From the shore came a shout: 'Jimmy?'

'Hello,' shouted I in return.

'We don't like the state of the river so we are keeping an all-night vigil on you from upstairs in the warehouse here.'

James and I were silent for a long time. 'What are you?' said he in the voice of one suddenly resigned to an eight-hour ordeal that was to rank among those of Scott, Hillary and, if we ran out of luck, Piccard.

'I have been thwarted yet again,' said I matter of factly.

'You have also been relegated to a very ex ex-friend if I ever get off this floating french letter alive,' said James, charged with emotion.

And so we passed the, as yet, most bizarre night of our lives. We didn't sink but it was the will of God which kept us afloat. Nor were we actually uncomfortable, but there was a final Chinese torture to come.

It was too dark to see our watches, plus the slightest movement caused us to dip and buck like a dolphin. There is a town clock in Bingley which chimes all night. Unfortunately the bloody thing doesn't, or didn't that night, chime the hour. The quarter, yes. The half and three quarters certainly. The ding dong chimes leading up to the hour strokes, oh yes. But may it rot and rust in hell, the strokes for whatever actual hour it happened to be, no! I went out of my mind calculating whether it was three o'clock or five o'clock. Or four o'clock or for any o'bleeding clock, but chime you bastard. But it never did and that is what really and truly exhausted me, so that when we were finally pulled in at dawn it was like I'd been adrift in the Atlantic for six years. But once again we lived to tell the tale and it's just another memory for when I get old.

A fat chance I've got of that. Having reached the stage in my quite unusual life where almost anything is possible places one in a strange situation. To work to live is now not necessary, nor has it been for some years. To work only for pleasure is not quite enough so I have to keep inventing reasons for doing things. While the Duchess was alive it was easy to just keep going. I kept earning money in case my Midas touch left me, as I didn't want her standard of living to drop. Now life has become a cheerful, sort of rudderless trip through quite calm waters. There is no shortage of projects for me for at the time of this writing I am handling about seventeen different personal efforts.

For instance, at Stoke Mandeville hospital where I am honorary entertainments officer, with my own room in the nurses' home no less, there's my mini-caravan camp. This was a scheme I started for paraplegic patients who needed a holiday while still under treatment. I got two new caravans and installed them on a most kindly and sympathetic site near Bournemouth, altering one of the vans to wide doors, movable beds, a ramp and intercom set. This van parked alongside a normal one meant that two patients, even up to totally disabled, could go to the seaside with either nurses or next of kin and have a normal holiday. Even pocket money was forthcoming if needed, from a fund I organized for that purpose. Even ambulance transport we can pay for. This project took about a year to fund and bring to an operating state. After a few seasons of smooth running I can hand over the whole shebang for some other organization to keep going. That provides me with a mild, necessary purpose to life. Also at the same hospital we realized, after many years, that some paraplegics with hand and arm motor muscle problems often had to get help to simply clean their own teeth. It was only the work of a couple of phone calls to get enough electric toothbrushes to set thirty of our patients free of help for this particular problem.

At Leeds Infirmary I started a separate radio deal for teenage patients. My fund there bought half a dozen big powerful radio sets with professional stereo headphones. Though we had, like most hospitals, the usual four-channel bedside radio headphones I suspected that young patients would like to dial the world of their own accord. The big sets I bought were about £100 each and you could almost get Australia. This proved very successful and I keep getting good-natured letters of complaint from parents who say their kids will only come home if they will buy them 'a big radio with earphones like Jimmy's'. The teen-type patients can keep these radios for as long as they are in hospital, and in several years we've never had one go missing. Of course lots of them have their own trannies but generally they are not the powerful short-wave type like mine. Particularly useful it was in the case of a girl from somewhere in Africa who communicated with no one, including the doctors, but who became quite relaxed after we found her own country's station on the dial. These things are great to do and keep me busy and useful enough.

Helping people is great fun but one can tend to get into complications at times. Driving down an icy road one winter

127

I noticed a sports car up a tree. Stopping to investigate I found a young guy covered in blood sitting on the kerb holding his head. Hauling him into my car I set off for the local hospital. It wasn't one of the three I work in but I knew it well enough. On the way I smelt strong booze so the lad had obviously had a few and come unstuck on the icy road. He was in enough trouble without the law claiming him as well so I tried a cover-up job. It was 3 a.m. and the hospital casualty was deserted. Carrying him into the examination room I started to clean him up, hoping his cuts were only superficial. Before I got very far an unsuspecting nurse came in and shot out of her shoes at this do-it-yourself scene. As it happens his injuries were enough to warrant a full-scale stitch job so I was promptly sacked.

'Leave the police call to me,' says I, 'I'll call in at the station and have his car picked up at the same time.' So far so good. Down to the cop shop. 'Hi,' says I. It was now 4.0 a.m. 'Just found a car up a tree, obviously an icy road job so I've taken the driver to the hospital.'

'Thanks,' said one of the law, 'I'll go up and see him.'

'Let me take you,' says I, 'don't feel like going to bed just yet.'

'O.K.,' says the law, and off we went.

On the way up I lit a big, foul cigar. Marching in to the casualty I gave it big puffs and said, 'How's my patient?'

The doctor went spare and ordered me and the policeman to kindly stand the other side of the curtain. Apologizing profusely I did so and the officer took the details as relayed by the doctor. Name, address, age etc. By having to stand ten feet from the patient it would have taken a drug-finder dog to detect the booze smell.

'Right doctor, thank you,' said the satisfied law, 'I'll pop back in the morning.' And off we went.

It was into bed for me and a good sleep, for I was to do a sponsored walk later that day.

Imagine who was waiting for me on my return to the finishing line. My police pal of earlier that night.

'Jimmy,' says he, 'congratulations.'

'For what?' says I, innocent like.

'If I ever get in trouble,' says the copper, 'I hope there's someone like you around to get me out of it.'

Knowing full well he'd sussed the score I kept schtum.

The lawman continued, 'Because when I went back this morning the lad was still drunk but I'd already made the report out and couldn't alter it could I.'

'Really,' says I, amazed, 'well, with me being tee-total—'

'Do me a favour,' says the super copper, 'you've topped me this time so I give you best. The cigar in the surgery was a great idea. Goodbye and a merry Christmas', and off he went.

I don't like taking a liberty with the law but sometimes you can't help it.

It reminds me of the time when I was running a dance hall in London. One of my local copper pals had just come back off his honeymoon to start night duty. 'I'll never last the night out,' says he about midnight. 'I'm shattered.'

'Right,' says I, 'come back about one and we'll both kip in the office and you can go off early and clock off.'

So we did. Him on the desk, me in the chair. At 6 a.m. he was away, with grateful thanks. Going down the dance hall to my changing room at the other end I found that, as we'd kipped, so we'd been burgled. I ring the cop shop and round come the day lads. Later that evening, as my recently married pal reports for his second night's duty, he is questioned by the inspector about if he saw anything suspicious round the dance hall seeing as it was on his beat. Little did the inspector realize that his staunch copper could hardly see anything downstairs or even outside seeing as he was fast asleep upstairs.

129

'Call in and see Jim,' says the inspector, 'and apologize to him for you not being there at the right time.'

'Right sir,' says my pal, white as a sheet at the fright of it all.

So didn't we have a laugh, and anyway it was only my stuff that had gone.

CHAPTER TEN

In an odd life one meets odd people. That I should instinctively like almost all people is a blessing with decided advantages.

Called upon to open a sale of work at a hostel for destitute men in Manchester, I went along some weeks before to reconnoitre the place. But I couldn't find it. The Morning Star Hostel for Destitute Men it was, in Nelson Street. After knocking on several doors I eventually got the right one. The obvious thing was that if I couldn't find it, our hoped-for customers would also search, tire and probably turn away. So I came up with a good idea. A pamphlet was printed which read 'Do you know where the Morning Star Hostel for Destitute Men is? No, well neither does Jimmy Savile but he will be sleeping there on Friday night to open a super sale of work there on the Saturday.'

We put the relevant dates on and a sketch map on the back. These bills were handed out in quantity and we finished up with a great throng. My night's kip there was a riot of earnest conversation, pong, snoring in all keys and volumes, and guests in long johns falling arse over tit down the stairs in the middle of the night.

With one of the lads I struck an immediate rapport. Ginger his name was and he had been many years in the Coldstream Guards. Six feet five he was and dressed in an enormous long coat on to which was pinned a small toy mouse and a mouth organ. When not holding a one-way conversation with the mouse, Ginger would serenade all within earshot on the mouth organ. Newspaper fastened round his legs, a large pin securing his coat and all this topped by an enormous shaggy ginger head and beard, he

131

was an awesome sight. A copious meths drinker he was, but we got on, for some reason, like twins: so much so I insisted he was on stage with me to declare the do open. At the last minute he got stage fright and fled the building. It was all a great experience for me and there was a super sequel about a year later.

It happened about 3.0 a.m. in the centre of sleeping Manchester. I'd just come down from my flat in Salford and was going into a disco, closed now, called Rails. Standing in the doorway sheltering from the night were half a dozen youths. These no-fixed-abode merchants abound in most big city centres. As it happens they are my pals like the rest of the world for they know that I started with not much and have been a bit lucky. On this night, one was dangerously drunk and, as with an animal, one had to beware. A face caked with dried blood told of an earlier conflict. A cheery 'evening gents' and I was inside.

It was about finishing in the disco so I was outside within fifteen minutes. The small team was still without and looking a bit sheepish as Mr Bloodyface waited on the pavement to do battle with anyone, me included. Walking out sideways so as to keep my wedding tackle away from the boot that invariably goes in first, I decided that a simple wrist-lock would be enough for a drunk. Waiting for him to make his move we all of us shot about six inches into the air as a great shout rent the night.

'Jim boy!'

For, padding down in his newspaper footwear, was the terrifying Ginger. In a single movement Ginger knocked my would-be antagonist into the middle of the road and seized my hand in a huge grip of friendship.

'What a surprise Jim boy,' he boomed.

An understatement to say the least, and no end of a relief as six to one is not my idea of good odds. The lads slunk off like jackals and left the two of us sitting on the wing of my

E-type smoking a cigar each. Ginger is dead and in heaven now and I'm sure looking forward to meeting up with him again when my time comes.

Another strange type it fell my lot to befriend was a single youth who worked as a glass-collector in a dive of a disco in London's Wardour Street. I had called in to give him a ticket for a film trade show and was stood at the top of the stairs talking to the solitary bouncer. Up the stairs marched four hoodlums. The leader produced a gun and said, 'Right, where's the wog bastard.' Who the wog gentleman was I shall never know but I trust he is enjoying better health than I was at that moment. There was momentary stalemate for this dramatic confrontation as both I and the petrified bouncer were decidedly Caucasian and certainly not wogs. Whatever they happen to be anyway. Into the middle of this still-life scene came my glass-collector pal. Simple but strong, he had biceps like footballs. He viewed the situation with some concern and said, 'What's wrong Jimmy?' I volunteered the information that we were possibly going to be shot. He disappeared.

But not for long, for he reappeared with a length of chain that could secure the Q.E.2. In total silence he flailed the chain at the surprised gunman and near on decapitated the poor chap. In their haste to leave, and complicated by the falling body of their leader, the other three fell down the stairs all arms and legs. My saviour laid into them with his fearsome weapon and there was much carnage. Bodies and blood spattered out into Wardour Street and the arrival of the law settled the fracas and all were bundled into the cop shop.

It was unthinkable that my pal could be left to his fate so we dispatched an irate barmaid round to Savile Row nick to ask why had they pulled her glass-washer off the job and he was just a spectator and if we couldn't have him back would someone be detailed off to come and clear the bleeding glasses and . . . So they let him go straight away which just goes to show it pays to be simple. The gun had disappeared to wherever guns disappear to in Wardour Street and I didn't go there much afterwards anyway.

My world is full of strange and wonderful people. Here the word strange is used in its nicest sense. Wonderful because they are just human beings more or less content with their lot.

It just occurs to me that I have not yet, overmuch, mentioned girls. Ah now, here we have a book on its own. It has never occurred to me to get married. There is no deep Freudian reason for this, nor is there any reason why I shouldn't. It's one of the few things I've just not got round to. It stands to reason that my type of business puts me up against, quite easily, thousands of girls. Great and momentous times we have had, the ladies and I. Monumental and magnificent. Tender, sometimes touching, but never turbulent. From single situations to team-handed times, girls have taught, trimmed and trained me up to Olympian standards. Think not that I would claim the ability to control and handle girls—like some foolish males would delude themselves. I have a disjointed sort of theory that all girls, in relation to their male opposites, are 2,000 years old when they are born. They might not know what makes a car go but they certainly have a very shrewd and intuitive idea as to what makes a man go. Or stop. I speak only within the framework of my experience. Not having been married, therefore never having to be constant or closely linked to any one for any length of time, girls have been part of the fun of living. Never having produced a child of my own, more by luck than management in the early days I fear, means that, like a summer's day, the girls of my world have always been something to look forward to.

Where do I start? At the beginning is a good place.

Sex education at my school was nil. On leaving at fourteen

134

I knew as much as when I started, which was nil. In retrospect this was no handicap for it never occurred to me that intercourse was at all important; it was just some strange, mysterious non-event. Even at such an early age, and because of my already working in a band after school, I was supposed to know all about it. One of my classmates came to me with the information that his sister had just given birth and he was inquiring after the mechanics of this house-shattering trauma. His sister was married so that made the explanation easy. 'It's simple,' I explained, 'her husband does it to her for an hour a night for nine months and she has a baby.'

'But she hasn't been married nine months, only five,' he countered.

My logical mind equated that it was a simple case of division and multiplication. 'Ah, then he did it to her for two hours a night for five months. It's the same thing.'

This eminently satisfied the both of us and we went out on our bikes.

My introduction to the sex act was, looking back, a masterpiece of ignorance and excruciating frustration for my unfortunate partner. I was, quite simply, picked up in the dance hall by a buxom and randy young lady for whom, that night, I was definitely the bottom of the barrel.

'Will you see me home?' said this despairing lovely. She realized, with her 2,000 years of intuition, that anything other than the direct approach would be totally lost upon me.

She lived a seven-mile train journey away. We were the only passengers in one of those carriages with no corridor. Once you were in you were in and no one could come along.

'Put your feet up on the seat,' she instructed.

So I did, but on the opposite one, not full length as she had meant. With a sigh that heralded the start of an exasperating night she rearranged me to her liking. Seats in those

135

third-class (remember them?) carriages were of modest width, and if only to save myself from falling to the floor I fastened hold of her ample form with some tenacity. Heartened by my firm grip she waited for the 'here it comes' and lay dormant. So did I.

Realizing that not only had she paid the fare, but she would also have to do all the work, she manhandled me into a sitting position and, to my terror mixed with embarrassment, slid her hand into my one and only pair of trousers and searched, in vain, for that which she hungered. We arrived at her station, Horsforth, in this somewhat Grecian pose, and it was time to alight.

We walked on in silence and I thought gleefully of what a super tale this would be for the lads, and I would definitely be Mr Big. My partner in delicious crime steered me round the back of her house. There was a private hedge shrouding a low wall, against which she leaned. Clutching me to her body like some flesh-eating plant, she once again started her search for the Nile. Oft times since have I tried to remember the details of our time in the bushes. Of one thing I am sure and that is I never took my arms from around her waist. Elsewhere was a mixed-up mystery of warmth, well being and discovery.

She spoke for the first time since leaving the train. 'I'm going now, will you be all right?'

'Yes,' said I, and not being able to think of anything else to say, 'I'm just going out on the bike tomorrow.'

She laughed a quiet little laugh and kissed me on the cheek.

I trotted home the seven miles and carefully committed each detail of this amazing night to my memory for subsequent discussion with the boys. From that day to this there have been trains and, with apologies to the hit parade, boats and planes (I am a member of the 40,000 ft club) and bushes and fields, corridors, doorways, floors, chairs, slag heaps,

136

desks and probably everything except the celebrated chandelier and ironing board.

As to the right and wrong of it, most of us have burned our bridges, not to mention our boats, long before we realize there could be a right or wrong to it. Ah that we were all but innocent animals. For fun, girls take a lot of beating.

But even in my game, where the girls abound like summer flowers, sometimes you lose. On stage at a concert in Scotland, with a packed audience only a few feet away, I suddenly became conscious of the fixed gaze of a girl in a blue wool dress. With the aid of discreet sign language I ascertained that she was indeed enamoured with me and not suffering from some eye trouble. In the hullabaloo of me finishing my stint I winkled her out of the crowd and into the calm lagoon of backstage. No, she didn't have to be home early, if at all. Yes, she had come to see me and certainly she would stick around until I'd finished with a press reception. 'Right,' says I, feeling great because she was a real darling, 'stay close.'

The route to the press room lay across a considerable expanse of exhibition hall. Security was strong and, surrounded by reporters and photographers, we made the comparative peace of the reception. Question, answer, and flash guns popped merrily and all was sunny, for did I not have a first-class mystery. A 'mystery', I would explain, is a young lady met but recently and therefore unknown.

After an hour of interrogation I thought it a decent time to take my leave. There were about fifty people in the room but, in growing horror, a decided shortage of blue wool dresses. When in doubt, ask a doorman. 'A girl in a blue dress, Mr Savile?' said a six foot six pillar of the Forth Bridge. 'Yes we had a lot of trouble with her, she said she was with you but we're used to those sort of tricks.'

The world suddenly became very grey at the edges. Explaining that she really *was* with me and where was she, out came the disaster story.

'She didn't have a coat or a press pass you see,' said the now much concerned doorman. 'We thought she was trying to pull a fast one. Kicked up a terrible fuss she did and it took two of us to put her out into the street.'

The grey edges of my world moved sharply inwards. 'How long ago was this?' says I with no hope.

'Over an hour' was the answer, 'and it's raining outside.'

In vain we rushed to the door. The street was dark, wet, and very empty, and mirrored my feelings to an exactitude. No name could be called into the darkness, like they would have done in a romantic film, but oft do I wonder what the blue wool dress would have looked like thrown over the back of one of my chairs.

Sometimes they are captured but you lose by the play of totally different forces. At a seaside town one dark and stormy night I drove on to the front to look at the wild waves. The sea road was closed for safety's sake as the waves were smashing in at over fifty feet high.

'Can I go through?' I shouted above the noise to the policeman in his wet oilskins. 'I want to record a few sounds.'

'Sure,' said the copper, 'with your luck if you get washed away you'd get washed back.'

And off I drove into the maelstrom of wind and water. A wild storm at sea viewed from the doubtful safety of the shore line, especially at night, is an awesome thing. Caught up in the majesty of it all, and with tons of water crashing on and all about the car, it was quite frightening. Suddenly my heart jumped into my mouth for, two inches away from my nose on the other side of the window, came a wild face with dark hair streaming across it. A small fist beat on the glass and a little voice shouted, 'Can I come and talk to you?'

It was a girl. From where she had sprung was of secondary

138

importance. That she would soon be gobbled up by the next wave was obvious. And here it came. Thousands of tons of it, fast as an express train. Opening the door, grabbing her in across me, and closing it, was two seconds and only just in time.

The inside of an E-type is not over capacious and just now seemed to be full of wet body, long black hair, legs and bikini panties. 'Lend me a comb,' says my five foot mermaid sorting herself out in the other seat.

Typically female; risk death but look good. Apparently she had been sitting in a car down at the barrier with her parents, seen me go through, jumped out, run along the sea road and here she was. Such a start had to mean a good night. Reversing back the five hundred yards to her folks' car she downed the window, said she was going off with me and would be back later. 'Right,' she instructed, 'let's go for a drive round, it's a super car.'

Should the reader feel that her folks appear unconcerned, you would not believe the stories I might tell you about some parents.

Anyway, off we went into the night. Talking, smoking and driving round in the night is a drop of the good life. From what I could see of her in the dark of the car she was a super looker. The steam started to come out of my ears but an E-type two-seater is not conducive to easy loving. Possible, with good friends mind you, but not to be recommended for first times. A diabolical plan formed within. Scarborough is the town in this story but my flat was out of the question for the Duchess was in residence and a sea-soaked girl across the threshold was unthinkable. However, I also had the Rolls in town, and not only was it in the garage but did not such drop-head Rolls have fold-back seats, grace and space? So off I steered with the excuse that sea water is bad for car bodies, which it is, and the Jag must be left for instant washing and we would transfer.

139

In retrospect it was at this point the job started going downhill. Once in the big car she examined all its mechanical wonders and started to go a little silent. The fall-back seats were a great success and, of course, seeing as I'd saved her from a watery grave she was duly appreciative. In the super silence of the afterwards and with lazy curling cigarette and cigar smoke, we spoke softly of this and that. About 4 a.m. we arrived outside her house. From the waves to the warmth it had been a tremendous night.

'I'll phone you next week,' says I.

'No you won't,' she replied in a strange quiet voice.

Nothing was more sure than that I would phone, because not only was the mixture as before most desirable but there were things like long journeys and weekends to think about. Out she climbed, shut the door and walked to the gate. Pausing, she turned back, opened the door, climbed in and kissed me one more once. And off she went.

A strange, super character thought I, driving back through the sleeping town. Actually I couldn't wait for the following weekend, for such is new romance. True to my word I dialled her number and there she was. The world was very rosy.

'I didn't think you'd phone,' says she in a small voice.

'So what time do I see you?' says I.

There was a silence. 'It won't work out,' she replied. 'People with money should stick to people with money so I can't see you again.' As an afterthought she added, 'I love you', and hung up.

My chameleon world promptly changed colour. A sort of shade of Scottish grey. All sorts of plans formed in my mind but one of the complications of being famous is that it's best not to pursue where the going could be turbulent because a famous life can get vastly more complicated than a normal one. She was as good as her word and left town that week to work away. For several years after I got Christmas cards with just her name and no address but they stopped eventually. I hope she is happy, and as for me, being twenty-four-hour busy has its advantages.

It is my theory that a man could work on stage with a nut and bolt through his neck like one of Frankenstein's monsters and some girl from the audience would fall for him. If he were to be clean, no bolt, and only just attractive at least ten per cent of the female audience would learn to fancy him after only a short time. Therefore someone madly handsome like me (!) collects at least twenty per cent of female fans at any one gathering. This is quite a conservative figure when one takes into account that at a concert by a living legend like Elvis or at a raving weenybopper show like the early Osmonds' the percentage can reach over the nineties.

Realize what this means in actual numbers. My average attendance figures in the dance halls for a seven night a week stint where I was the overall boss as well as the main disc jockey, was about one thousand. That means that at least two hundred girls per night would take kindly to any suggestions I might make. If half of those were shy and gazed only from afar and only half of the remainder were a little bold, that means that on any one night at least fifty girls would actually do the chatting up. To be even more conservative, if I only fancied half of the fifty, that left twenty-five super dolly birds actually putting the pressure on me, or any of my disc jockeys. With such quite reasonable statistics it follows that trouble with a capital T, pleasure with an equal capital, and just about everything else in between, comes in large quantities. And that's only for personal appearances. Multiply those figures by the millions who watch TV or listen to the radio and life gets interesting or complicated according to your state of health.

The social dangers of such temptations are immense. At 2 a.m. one morning there came a small knock on my door in Manchester. Standing there was a young, super-shape girl.

141

About seventeen or eighteen I estimated. Manchester is a big city and such things can happen.

'I saw your light on,' she said, and stood there waiting for her chemistry to take effect on me.

Normally such manna would be consumed but my guardian angel works, thank goodness, a twenty-four hour shift.

'I'm just going out,' says I with great effort and cursing myself for being chicken, 'but I'll be back in an hour.'

Such King Solomon decision gave me an each-way bet. Leaving her sitting on the step I was off to town in the car. Fifty yards down the road I get stopped by a police car. 'That girl just gone into your block is an absconder,' says the law.

'What girl?' says I.

'Lucky boy,' says the law, and zooms off to claim the runaway. Such eleventh-hour escapes reduce one to a jelly.

Being part coward I've always had a lively horror of being caught at anything and this has doubtless saved my life on many occasions. Hiding in cupboards or outside on fire escapes has kept peace where there would have been conflict. Once, in London, I had a girl delivered to me in a sack. It was far too heavy to lift from the outside step and I got a touch of the horrors in case the body, for it was obvious to the feel, was dead. It wasn't but it was also unnecessarily melodramatic because it was broad daylight and one doesn't feel half as guilty during the day.

Near heart failure when caught is also an occupational hazard. I had once been invited by six young ladies to their holiday caravan for a late-night visit. Off we went in high fun mood, all seven of us packed into my three-wheel bubble car. Half the caravan had been made into an enormous bed and we all lounged upon it. Four a.m. and strong salt sea air make a lethal sleeping draught and in no time we were all unconscious. Came suddenly a large knocking on the door. Immediately awake and nervous at unfamiliar surroundings,

142

a scene of human collapse met the eye. The heat of the albeit innocent night had caused the girls to shed the majority of their day clothes. In some cases all. I had started off wearing a black leather suit but this had been cast aside. We all resembled some great sleeping human octopus. Again the peremptory knock. One of the girls arose from the human pile like Venus. Peering out of the curtain she suddenly became rigid with fright and disbelief.

'It's my mother and father,' she hissed.

In a twinkling there was a silent movie pandemonium. Escape was uppermost in my mind but that was impossible for I can vouch to the fact that when six girls plus clothes and suchlike move into a holiday caravan there remains not enough room to hide a toe let alone a five foot nine body. A further complication was that my leather trousers had become folded and crinkled. Trying to force my legs into these convolutions, and buffeted by six girls all panic-stricken and searching for necessary garments, was a situation of no-escape horror. After an age we opened the door. The girls were draped around the walls of the van like some female equivalent of the St Valentine's Day massacre.

'Come in,' called I in a cheery voice, not being helped by the fact of just jamming my feet into shoes in which a sock had inadvertently been left in each, so my insteps were arched like a defensive tom cat. 'Hope you're not looking for breakfast. I've been here half an hour but these ladies don't function well in a morning.'

Heaven be praised, the parents stood for it and admonished their daughter for being tardy to the needs of guests. Eventual escape, scot free, was like being re-born and I vowed never to bat on an away pitch ever again.

How futile are our vows when fate dictates otherwise. It was only a little later that fine summer day when trouble loomed again. Walking across the sands with two minders, Barry and Roy, and wearing a floppy hat as disguise, I am

143

spotted by an eagle-eye sirene. She falls in alongside, peers under the hat and says, 'Ha, it is you.' She is in a one-piece swimsuit and looks good enough to eat. 'Come and meet my parents over here,' she says, taking my arm.

I am not unwilling to be led away, or astray for that matter, and we all finish up sitting on the sand. 'Where are you staying?' is my polite inquiry.

'In a caravan,' says mum and dad.

A faint chill blows across my soul.

Daughter jumps to her feet. 'Come and look inside, it has leaded windows,' she cries.

Wild horses would not have got me into another situation similar to my recent deliverance but this chick was in no way resembling a horse. Wild or otherwise. With her bare feet in the sand, legs straining to pull me up, tanned body and corn hair, she took me in tow like a zombie.

Leaving mum and dad with Barry and Roy we crossed the road to a modest holiday van. Inside, the temperature is nearly 100 degrees. If the van had suddenly gone into orbit, ten miles high, for the afternoon, then doubtless my courage would have overcome my qualms. As it was, my qualms were having a field day and I jumped a mile at every near footstep.

'Are you going into town later?' says my kidnapper.

'Sure,' says I, fighting a losing battle with my tummy muscles.

'Good, you can give me a lift. I'll just change.'

Locking the outside door she retreats to the gloom of the far end of the caravan. I have sunk into a chair, wringing wet with the heat and temptation. A rustling and snapping from the dark end tells me that the swimsuit is off. At that precise moment, and I swear before God and witnesses it was at that very precise moment, the outside door handle gave a click, turn and pull. Mum and dad had come across to join us.

'Jesus, Mary and Joseph,' breathes the girl, obviously Jewish. 'Don't let them in yet.' Her problem seemed to be

144

that an elastic swimsuit when not in use resembles the inside of a golf ball, and about as big.

To find necessary leg holes and corresponding armholes is a job best done with time to spare. Should one attempt to hurry this operation one finishes up executing a one-leg dance. Under normal circumstances this doesn't matter and, if watched by lawful husbands, is even perhaps funny. Alas, my normal humour was dormant unto death. Within, there was a naked young lady stomping up and down on one leg; without was mum and dad claiming rightful admittance. The temperature inside the van on this hot afternoon was now well over the hundred and the water was running off the both of us. Three things I did at the same time: prayed that I might simply disappear, put a comic magazine over my head, and reached out to unlock the door. The blast of hot air from inside the van caused mum to step backwards onto dad.

'Pooh, the heat,' says mum as she makes it inside. From the far end gloom comes the voice of daughter.

'We had to keep the curtains closed else he'd been snowed under for autographs.'

I was near on passed out in the chair under my comic and uttered not a word. The situation had been saved by daughter sliding like an eel into a slip of a dress, minus undies, and pretending to make tea. I was finished. But really finished. Twice delivered in but one day was just too much and I was robbed of movement and speech so I feigned sleep.

Eventually it was business as usual but friends will tell you that since that day I never, ever, operate outside my own four walls. As I have a considerable number of four walls dotted about the country, life is not too restricted.

It has never occurred to me to get married. At least not yet. It must be very pleasant to have a sort of female best pal that you can share things with during the day and keep each other company during the night. Rushing about like I do and taking the marrow of ambrosia out of what my part of the world has to offer doesn't give me the time or inclination to settle down. Sometimes, totally exhausted after days of charity walks and nights of similar appearances, I have to re-assess if I'm doing the right thing. Thinking of the guys I know with dolly wives at home, with telly, tea and fire, maybe I'm missing out after all.

A lot of my things turn into yearly events. The taxi outings to Blackpool, Worthing and Southend I've been on from five to ten years and it would come hard to break the habit. Nine years I've done the big Dublin walk for the Central Remedial Clinic. Who could not want to walk with 35,000 great Irish teentypes? Ten years with this priests' affair, eight years of the Little Sisters of the Poor walk, and so on and so on. In all there's about thirty different annual affairs that come hard to break. If public friendship changes and I stop drawing the crowds the answer would be simple. The alternative life of going back to being anonymous doesn't worry me at all for the world is full of things to enjoy, but it doesn't seem quite right to decide to call a halt to this ceaseless round. I think it's one of those things left to the will of the Good Lord. When He thinks enough is enough then that'll be good enough for me. Who knows, He might send some 'female best pal' along and I'd join the golden ring gang. To get married I'd rather leave the business as it's not easy to be faithful at one end of the country if you have a wife waiting at the other. By now I suspect I'd not be much of a prize as a husband. Leaving it too long and getting set in one's ways of being self-reliant is possibly not the best start to a life of twosome harmony.

CHAPTER ELEVEN

Thank goodness it takes all sorts to make a world. One of the nicest spin-offs of my sort of life is that my path lies right across the paths of Kings, Queens, Princes, Presidents—and the penniless. Genuine aristocracy is a joy. They live a sort of 'arms length' life from everybody else, and why not? Crowns and Coronation Street don't mix, just like different engine oils don't, but they can certainly have a good time together.

Prince Philip was top tabling a do at London's Lyceum ballroom. I was on the next table and the only showbiz person there. Our guests were 2,000 bingo players, mainly ladies, from all over the country. Such a night it was, from old-time war songs to community singing, and we all of us stayed right to the end singing and eating and clapping. But even at the height of the fun no one dreamed of taking a liberty with the prince.

With Angus Ogilvy and his super missus Princess Alexandra one feels a great friendship from the off. I am the vice-president to his presidency of the National Association of Youth Clubs and he is often down with us at headquarters in Devonshire Street, wanting to know what's happening. Princess Alex is a patron of a hostel for girls in care. At this place I'm a cross between a termtime boyfriend and a fixer of special trips out. The Princess is a natural for such a place. Girls in care don't take kindly to royal rules, protocol and the like, but Alex just steams in, captures them and anyone else that's around, and steams out.

Invited one day to tea with the Queen Mother at St James's Palace, it was all very nice and chatty and fun. After Queen Mum had gone the guests trickled away. We were in the throne room at the time and the Most Important Seat was roped off with golden cords. As it happens the ropes were only eighteen inches from the ground and offered no barrier. Having done most things but not yet sat on the Throne of England, the temptation was too much. All had gone save a handful. No one was looking. Treason or not, it was too good to miss. A quick step over the rope and gentle sit down. There may have been other short-lived occupants of that throne but none with such an eyes-closed and blissful smile as mine. I thought of knighting myself while I was there but I didn't have the sword.

As a hobby I am quite interested in millionaires. Especially multi ones. Having quite enough loot of my own doesn't alter the fact that, to me, other people with real oodles of the stuff are quite fascinating to just study. An odd hobby perhaps but it's not far removed from tropical fish or an aviary. Paul Getty, who doesn't know me from Adam, I used to meet on occasions at the Mr Universe body-building show. I've never quite fathomed out why he accepted our invitation. I'm the President of the Association, but come along he did, in a mile-long black Cadillac. Pale of face and hands and courteous as only an American can be, he would arrive and depart quietly. People say he looked morose but that's not strictly true. Come to think of it, there's not many people around that look like the laughing policeman.

I have a friend in Tangier who lives in a palace. Seventy-five candles burn in his entrance hall. Guests arrive by jet and yacht and when I'm there my thoughts, some of the time, stray back to the Morning Star Hostel for Destitute Men in Manchester. It's a strange world all right, and seeing as we'll never quite straighten it out in our lifetime, there's not much harm in enjoying it. As long as it's not at the expense of others.

One of the most onerous chores of being well known is signing autographs. The principle of autographs is quite

148

complimentary but the act is doubtless the most off-putting feature of showbiz. It would be really nice to go to open a fête, look people in the eyes, shake their hand and have a short chat. That I could do willingly all day and every day. The way it works is quite different. One could spend easily the whole day, head down seeing nothing, and signing impossible bits of paper that are promptly lost. Pens that don't work, and paper, thin as tissue, that you couldn't write on anyway, or beermats with no space round the advert for legible writing: it consumes endless hours and is usually a terrible free for all. Nevertheless it is an enormous compliment that one human being should want a souvenir of another. At leisure it's a pleasure but in crowds it's the thing that causes me to look for the back door.

With autographs there is no mercy and nothing is sacred. The greatest example of this must be when I was bringing the body of my darling Duchess home to Leeds from Scarborough. I was travelling up front in the hearse so as to be nearby and, of course, each mile was a memory. Just outside Leeds the two undertakers with me in the front, naturally embarrassed but mortally afraid of going back to their kids without a signature, produced two autograph books. Actually it did me a favour for it reminded me that, grief or no grief, life has to go on for those left behind. So better realize it sooner than later.

Another quite unique occasion was during a fell race. These most punishing of foot races usually take place in the Lake District. The competitors set off from a central field during a gala, and run up the local mountain, usually grass-covered with an average gradient of one in two, or three. These are killer races. I had trained well for this one, up Latrigg Fell near Keswick, and was lying thirteenth about two hundred yards from the leaders. Making my effort round the finishing track and running through a narrow corridor of spectators, you wouldn't believe but about five hundred

149

yards from the line a man jumped out, right in my path, and thrust an autograph book in my face with the totally impossible remark, 'Just sign this Jimmy.' Unable to stop I crashed into him and we both went down. Totally exhausted from running up and down the mountain and with now no chance of catching the leaders I could have wept with rage and disbelief.

Several times I've been knocked off for illegal parking, and quite rightly so, but it's a laugh when the warden waits around for an autograph before carrying on his way. Several times I've not been knocked off when I should have been and the warden still waits for a signature. That's even better.

Yet another facet of being well known is the ability to get out of the way on occasions. It's more novelty than popularity that causes people to crowd round a well known face. Several journeys have I spent in train toilets so as not to be an added aggravation to several hundred football supporters on the same journey. The last thing that quiet passengers in my compartment want is legions of boisterous whatever trampling them underfoot.

Possibly my greatest escape was in a university. The atmosphere of such academic seats suits me for they are full of inquiring and active people. One such university came to me because their annual charity rag was running into trouble for lack of ideas. We formed a small committee of six. I warned the guys that I was a hard taskmaster. For six weeks I rode them and the general students hard. The rag was a huge success and took record money, with every stunt a well organized winner. It was a unanimous plea that I make an appearance at the college buildings, in London, to speak to all, after. My original but now exhausted committee came to collect me. They were strangely quiet. Always hypersensitive to atmosphere I sussed all was not well. Not knowing why, I took a Colombo style old raincoat with me instead of my usual more expensive one. On the journey to the college the reason for their reticence came clear. I was in for a debagging. The vulgarity of success is never more obvious than in universities. As I had spearheaded a successful rag by riding roughshod over all, I was to be given the final honour. Rather like being thrown in the river after winning the boat race.

Whilst I am in favour of even de-bagging myself in certain soft and scented circumstances, a union stage is not the place I would choose. So here was to be a classic of getting out of the way. Great plans had been made. After my speech there was to be a sonic bang of huge proportions engineered by the engineers. Flash powder had been scattered along a metal channel running the length of the stage. This was to be ignited simultaneously with the bang and, as a final touch, the mains electric switch would be thrown to plunge the hall into temporary darkness. Only then were the 2,000 students at liberty to fall upon my frail and supposedly surprised form.

The union hall beggared description. A vast mob of students, armed with fire extinguishers and other assorted fun weapons of mayhem, seethed about the floor. Behind me on stage sat thirty members of this fine body in a row and, just to finish it off, the rugby team were equally divided on either side of the wings. It was the stuff of which the celebrated Mr Bond almost gets his comeuppance in his films. Arriving at the side door my mind was going like a rat in a cage. Going back to my villain days I automatically appraised each window, door, passage and corridor as I walked to the execution chamber.

Going on stage the noise was deafening. My words were listened to with good grace for we were all friends. And so came the end of my speech. A roar of acclaim from the throats of all was drowned by the stupendous BANG. Out went the lights and the flash powder made blinding light and

151

white smoke. On went the lights, forward surged the mob.

The stage was empty and I had simply disappeared. An illusion was never so electric. One second I was there. The next, all that was left was an old raincoat.

The pandemonium was immense. Cheated of their victim they all raged about the building. Considerable superficial damage was done to walls and windows with water and foam. Chairs were smashed and doors were splintered as the 2,000 students raved through the union.

So where was I? Well, it was like this. First of all I badly needed lady luck and she turned up on time, as always in my life. Arriving on stage I had insisted on being introduced properly. A chair had been brought and I placed it right in the middle of the thirty strong committee row behind me. Getting up to speak left my empty chair. At the end of the speech followed by the bang, flash, and two-second darkness was exactly when I did a back somersault over my empty chair. This left me in line with the join of the stage curtain. Through it in a twinkling I was. With the lights on and pandemonium at my miraculous disappearance, all it took was a quick sprint across the back of the curtain, out through the door in the wings, down two short corridors and, of course, into the ladies' loo. Locking myself into a cubicle and sitting with my feet up against the door it was fingers crossed and pray. (A technical point here. When taking refuge in a ladies' loo it behoves one to elevate the feet for those who would peer beneath the door, as a pair of big male shoes gives the game away.) It's the first time I've ever been incognito in a ladies' loo and it's quite interesting.

For an hour I stayed still, listening to the sounds of pursuit die down. Several times groups of ladies charged in to, as it were, dwell on the facilities, and talk about where I was. There was a keen sense of disappointment at being deprived of the anticipated sight of my wedding tackle. When all was quiet it was short work to be out, down the passage and into a providentially passing taxi. Of such occasions are the good laughs of life made. But only afterwards.

Escapes like that have been few and far between, as I consider the necessity to escape generally the result of bad personal organization. Organization is the machinery that manufactures the good life.

On my almost lifelong and often lonely travels, either in my various Rolls Royces or on foot during my many marathon marches, I often get to musing on the fifty-four million people of this country of ours. My present life's spectrum runs from dead bodies in the middle of the night to riotous times in schools with children. From down and outs to the up and coming, right through to all the people at the top. Intimate contact with people of all these groups gets me to working it all out. A fascinating thing to do. Hopelessly impossible, but fascinating. St Paul, wandering on the beach, pondered on the same thing about the Holy Trinity. He didn't make it either. Not a bad policy is to do nothing, wait until something happens, then organize it as cleverly as you can. Most times I've tried to accomplish something from scratch. It's been like swimming against the tide of life. Yet we are all apparently compelled to get up and do something. Frustration, exhaustion, and that old is-it-worth-it feeling is an almost automatic follow up.

I am walking across a high mountain pass in Scotland. A shepherd waits by the road with his dog.

'How far is it to so-and-so?' I ask.

'Not too far,' he says.

'How many miles?' I persist.

'Not sure,' says he, 'never really worked it out.' He pauses and looks across the mountain. 'About half a day,' is his final decision.

The village in question was eighteen miles away. He had lived in the area all his life and didn't know. A fabulously simple life and almost to be envied, but impossible for nearly all of us because of this compulsion to get up and do something. Only the very young, the very old, and the shepherds, have the secret.

I say, wouldn't it be a great idea if we all had two separate goes at life? Forget the spiritual theories for the moment. Imagine we all could come back again, remembering the wisdoms of our first time round, and we were all given a second chance. Or would it be the same? Would the personal mistakes still be made that hold us captive to the system? The violent crime of momentary passion that gets people locked up for life. The temptation that puts you outside the law of society, brands you, and affects you till you die.

At Stoke Mandeville hospital, when I help the lads on nights and wheel away the dead bodies from the wards of the older patients, I look down at them and wonder. What had these lovely old folks, who have just done with life, learned about it? What secrets of wisdom have died with them? Is there really such a thing as wasted days or years? As I push them through the night air to our outside mortuary I can see the stars. What's it all about? Whatever it's all about we're all well and truly stuck with it, so if we're compelled to get up and do things, until we die, we might as well enjoy it if we can. If we have to answer for our lives after death, those people who have made other people unhappy will be the ones really in trouble with the Boss.

In the never-ending interviews I give, one question keeps cropping up. 'When will it all end?' That's the big question in our candyfloss pop business. The average big-time life of groups, singers and suchlike is about two years. There are many exceptions to this rough rule but I can look back over ten years of Top of the Pops scripts and see many big names now long forgotten. So how long my own scene lasts is a fair question. At the time of this writing, 1974, my own show's always spectacular listening, viewing and reading figures have, even just now, shot up into the phenomenal. Savile's Travels one-hour show on Radio One has already run for seven years, uninterrupted. The latest listening figures have actually overtaken the enormous Family Favourites' on Radio Two. An incredible feat.

Speakeasy, another one-hour talk show of mine, comes via the Religious Department of the B.B.C. This show is unique as it is the only talk show on Radio One in the whole week. Its enormous listening figure, one week, even surpassed Savile's Travels. Speakeasy has been running for six years and, in the words of one top B.B.C. man, 'We want this show to continue for ever!'

Top of the Pops on TV is the world's longest running all-pop show. I did the first one ten years ago and we're both still going strong. During the decade of this quite phenomenally successful show I've been through every phase of the pop scene since, of course, 1964.

My own weekly column in the *Sunday People* has been going for twelve years: sometimes only 300 words, sometimes 6,000. I love writing for the paper and my bit is always well up in the early pages.

My own annual TV series is called Clunk Click. I borrowed the title from the nickname I acquired from the seatbelt commercials I did for I.T.V. These commercials were so successful that they won seven major TV awards in one year. Both in Britain and abroad!

After ten years at the top and winning some forty odd personal no. 1 awards my present wage-pulling power stuns even me. For a half-hour appearance at the 1974 Ideal Home Exhibition I raked in £50,000 which I promptly gave to Stoke Mandeville Hospital. A TV commercial later that year grossed me £130,000. Again I gave it, or most of it in this case, promptly away. My reasoning was that if I didn't need it, thank God, there's no point in keeping it. If nothing else, such a chronicle of success answers the question of 'how long will it last'. The answer is, of course, 'long enough for me!' A quick look at my long-running B.B.C. shows. On radio, Savile's Travels is beautiful in its simplicity. Asked by the Corporation to give them a pop record show, I simply collected a pocket tape-recorder, thrust it up the nose of all the marvellous and strange people I meet, selected a list of records to go in between the chat bits and, hey presto, a winner.

Speakeasy is a much different kettle of fish. (I've never found out why they should keep fish in a kettle.) Several years ago a priest from the B.B.C. Religious Department rushed into my dressing room at Top of the Pops and said, 'Jimmy, I've got one hour of time on Radio One, what are we going to do with it?' Within thirty minutes we had knocked out the format that still held good seven years later. Again simple. Take any subject from cancer and death to politics and dreams. Collect a couple or so experts and an audience of 300. Two roving mikes to pick up the opinions of the audience and, again, another winner. We also do 'specials'. These speakeasys are held in a small intimate studio, with maybe thirty specialised audience, and we discuss and broadcast things like—homosexuality and what it means to be one. Or there's a jolly crowd of the deaf. Or the blind. Once a collection of thirty different foreigners on what it was like to be a foreigner in Britain. These chat shows were unique in so far as I never looked for argument, because that wastes a lot of time in defence, only the opinions of a cross-section of the public. The listeners made up their own minds.

Some beautiful moments were had on this show. On the subject of divorce I asked a lady had there been any one thing that caused the breakdown of her marriage. 'I think,' she pondered, 'it was when the au pair girl first became pregnant.'

On one on birth control I asked another lady, who had

156

tried everything, why she chose the pill when she really favoured the condom. 'I think,' she also pondered, 'when I first realized I was allergic to rubber.'

On our panel of experts once, we had a titled lady of over eighty. Wanting to smoke a cigar but not wishing to distress her (sitting next to me), I leaned across and whispered, 'Will my cigar smoke bother you?'

A little hard of hearing, she replied, 'It's very good of you but I'll have one of my own.'

I nearly fell off the chair as this darling eighty-year-old pulled out a cigar case and had hers lit while my mouth was still open.

Cabinet ministers, bishops, archbishops, M.P.s, lords, ladies and gentlemen have all readily agreed to come on our Speakeasy programme.

For years B.B.C. TV, suggested I should do my own TV series. Not only did I not press the question, I actually avoided it. Too much can be too dangerous and I was always quite content to be on Top of the Pops for as long as it would run. My logic was, as usual, simple. My exposure on there was about two minutes out of thirty. As I did it about twice a month that meant four minutes on TV in four weeks. Not much, you would say. Enough, I would venture, for in that four minutes with my weird outfits and hairstyles I earned enough impact to last easily a month. Therefore what more could be gained by going on the telly for fifty minutes a week. Only a fifty to one chance of getting into trouble, that's all. It had to come however, and one day our Light Entertainment boss, the famous Bill Cotton, summoned me to his room.

'You will do your own TV show for thirteen weeks, peak time, Saturday evening, from next May,' he barked.

'Thank you,' says I.

Bill looked at me in astonishment. 'You'd never do it before.'

'Before,' said I, 'you always asked me, this time you've told me.'

So me and a big team had big fun making some big shows. I'd tell you what they were except that they were about everything and that's not easy to describe. Almost like a pictorial Savile's Travels, they would include everybody from a gentleman who blew up, and burst, hot-water bottles, to a 103-year-old superman who had just, in the previous six months, been up in a hot air balloon, gone round a race track at 160 m.p.h., driven a juggernaut lorry, and who collapsed ten million people by saying, 'I've had a much better time in the last three years than I did in the first hundred!'

Sometimes I think there's nothing else for me to do or win, but something crops up. In 1973 I won the world's top award, the Variety Club of Great Britain Showbiz Personality Award. That's it, thought I, it's impossible to top that. And felt a bit sad. The next year, and it just had to be an Irish award, I was voted no. 1 disc jockey. 'So,' you might ask, 'you've already got over forty such awards.' 'Sure,' says I, 'but they can't even hear Radio One in Ireland,' (Well in the south anyway.) I asked the man from the magazine who presented the award how they worked it out. 'Sure Jimmy,' he says, 'we don't have to hear you to know you're the top.' And you can't top that.

As for new things to do. It occurred to me that I'd walked the length of the country, and cycled back up again—so I set off one day and ran across. From the Cumberland coast to the North Sea. About 130 miles and it was a laugh a mile. We filmed it for Nationwide and it took me four days 'cos running 130 miles is not easy, but it sure is fun with a film crew and half the population of the North of England taking part.

Strange happenings follow me around like a shadow. This can cause people to think that I am possessed by spirits, good

158

or bad. For instance, on my second trip to Fort William in Scotland my local pal, Jim Rogers, took me out to Mallaig. On the way back he made a detour so I could meet one of the great characters of the Highlands. Old Donald was his name and he lived by the side of Europe's deepest lake, Loch Morar. 'If Old Donald likes you,' said Jim, 'we might persuade him to play his fiddle.' A great local honour. Me and this great old character got on well from the off. After a cup of tea, down came the fiddle and the fun started. Twenty minutes of honest music ended with a riotous reel. Old Donald and I held the floor, he playing, me jigging. The reel finished and we bowed to each other. I looked into his crystal-clear eyes—and he fell dead at my feet. Stunned, destroyed and entirely disbelieving I tried for half an hour to revive him. To no avail. Old Donald had gone to heaven a happy man surrounded by his music and the people he loved.

Jim and I drove on back to Fort William, both of us subdued. 'I promised my parents we'd call and say hello,' said Jim. His folks were old and very nearly chair-ridden by the open fire. I was, as always in Scotland, wearing the kilt. For a laugh I stood in front of the fire and hitched up the kilt at the back. 'Ahh,' says I, 'that feels good.' So we had a laugh and left. As Jim and I drew into my hotel, the famous Milton a fire siren sounded down in the town. It had to be my fault what happened. We had been out of his parents' house only a few minutes when all the soot cascaded down the chimney and set the carpet ablaze. His folks escaped by showing a miraculous turn of long-forgotten speed, into the garden. After this, Jim gave me long pensive glances but didn't actually voice his fears.

Some things happen in threes. That night we went to a local club. It was a night of great gaiety. As I left, one of the older members suddenly climbed on to the stage, drew a mouth organ from his pocket and proceeded to play. 'Stand still,' hissed Jim. 'It's old Bob' (I think that was his name) 'and he's playing you a lament.' So like it was the National Anthem we both stood there. As the lament drew to a close I raised one arm on high as a salute. The fine old gent stood straight as a ramrod and gave me a similar, silent salute in return. As we left Jim explained that, like Old Donald playing the fiddle unasked, so this latest was a gesture of local appreciation not given to many, to say the least.

The following morning I was on a charity walk, the object of my visit. On the line, surrounded by all the local guys and gals and just about to set off, up comes Jim with a dark face.

'They've found old Bob's pipe,' said he.

'Great,' says I cheerfully, 'how long had he lost it?'

'They've found old Bob's pipe,' said Jim, keeping his distance, 'but they haven't found Bob.'

Off I had to go, in considerable turmoil. Was this the third? It was. This fine old gentleman had, after playing me his salute, put the mouth organ in his top pocket, went out, and accidentally fell in the adjacent Caledonian Canal! They found him the following day. I felt it best to leave the Fort a day early ere I denude the Highlands of all their old folks.

An incredible P.S. to this quite disturbing saga, and believe it because it's perfectly true, was this. Leaving a day early gave me time to spare so I phoned a girl I knew in Glasgow. 'Meet me off the train,' says I. 'Great,' says she, and we arranged to call and see the family of a joint friend of ours. It was a date of long-standing promise. On the way to the house, me suitably disguised as it was daytime, I got the low-down on the family. 'My dad can be a bit grumpy because he sleeps downstairs in a chair since years,' says the joint friend. 'He's got rheumatics in the neck and the pain makes him bad-tempered.'

So I finish up in a nice little house on a Glasgow scheme chatting away to this fine man and his great family. My hospital work makes me interested in pain so I question him. As it happens I think I can help. In my bag I usually carry a tube of very good balsam ointment that we wrestlers use to keep us mobile after a pulled muscle. Doubtful of it being any good for him, but wanting to humour this strange friend of his daughter's, he lets me put some on his neck and shoulders. After a few minutes he looks at me in amazement. 'It works,' says he, in a wondering voice, 'the pain's gone.'

To say we were all amazed, and me jubilant, was to put it mildly. In a great state of congratulation we parted. I made him a present of my tube of wonder gunge. He stayed by the fire and lit his pipe. We all went off, the ladies to the bingo and me to catch the train to London. I swear to God this is true but how I wish it hadn't happened. The old man, relieved of pain after so many years, fell asleep in the chair, out fell his pipe, set fire to the house, and burned him to death. When I was phoned with the news I couldn't believe it. My four-day trip in my beloved Scotland had cost three sudden deaths and two near misses. Pure coincidence no doubt, I hope, but in certain areas I am now regarded with the same degree of respect as a witch doctor with the evil eye.

To round off this, not the happiest of subjects, I once went into an old folks' home run by the nuns. Great was the excitement and the kissing. In the middle of all this, one of the old ladies had a heart attack and took a mortal swoon in our midst. I was terribly upset and the Mother Superior, in an effort to placate me, made the quote of all time. 'Never mind Jimmy, we were very overcrowded anyway.'

So as you can see, my life runs from the fiasco of fun, to triumph, and right across the spectrum to tragedy. I seem to sail through it all like a boat bobbing on the waves. Often I wonder why I am never moved to any *great* emotion. Standing before a vast screaming happy crowd I experience a feeling of gentle love for them. Watching the life ebb out of one of my hospital patients, along comes the same warm, wondering feeling. Dawn or dusk, with Venus in the sky, there it comes again.

Talking, one day, to the consultant in our casualty department at Leeds Infirmary (I'd not been doing voluntary work there long), he spoke briefly on a phone. 'Come with me,' he says. 'I'll show you some real tragedy.' What was left of a coalminer after being caught up in the coal-cutting machine was being laid out on an emergency table. Not a pretty sight. He was still conscious but in silent shock.

'Hello,' says I.

'Hello Jimmy,' says he.

I look at his crushed legs. The consultant makes his preparations and watches me with one eye. The man's bent legs, bent the wrong way, must be straightened first. Speed is the essence. Knowing it to be right I hold the miner's face in my two hands.

'If you'd worked down my pit this would never have happened,' says I.

He smiled, then fainted at the shock of the straightening.

My doctor friend, for we grew into good friends, was giving me a baptism into the world of tragedy. Apart from feeling the stubble on the miner's face I felt little else, except my familiar warm, reaching out sensation. From then on I was trusted with anything and everything. I hasten to add that most hospital workers deal with this sort of event every day, but it comes as a surprise for them to see a disc jockey there in the middle of life and death. Or it used to come as a surprise to them. It doesn't anymore.

It has been put to me by an eminent man of wisdom that my mixture of clairvoyance, instinct and intuition is because, having been over the rim of death as I told you at the start of this book, one always brings something extra back. I don't know if he's right or wrong, but whatever it is, it's worked for me a good life.

162

CHAPTER TWELVE

Most autobiographies are written at the end of someone's life. This one is not like that because long after the date of publication I have lots of big new things planned. Like a special in-depth tour of the Black Sea ports and the far end of the Mediterranean basin. Like also for years all sorts of American interests have wanted me to go there for TV work and lecture tours of American colleges. I have a permanent open offer to wrestle in Japan. Australia, New Zealand and other antipodean paradises send messages with visiting TV chiefs. 'Tell us when you're going to be around Jim and we turn on the studio lights.' I am in the process of designing a mini motor caravan so I can live in the more remote parts of even this country. For there are still remote parts of Britain, beyond the mighty motorways. So really, all I've gone through up to press is just the groundwork for the big push. Or it could be that, just opting out of the normal marriage-mortgage-kids complex, I can live six lives with ease.

Whichever way it is, as long as we can still laugh at things, each other, or ourselves, we'll get by.

Laughing at ourselves is a great tonic. Once, early in my career, I was driving down Oxford Street in Manchester in my big car and feeling quite good about it. I am waiting at the traffic lights and a drunk walks over the crossing. He stops and sways gently, looking at me. Walking up to my open driver's window he plucks the cigar from my mouth, turns it round and sticks the lighted end in first. At that moment I am just easing the car forward. By a drunken miracle he has scored a bull's eye and the lighted end has gone in my mouth with no burning damage en route. If I suddenly brake I will get the car behind in my boot, and I dare not try to spit the cigar out for the red end of a big cigar carries unspittable quantities of molten ash. So I have to drive across to the Midland Hotel corner with smoke coming down my nose and tears in my eyes. The slight burn I suffer cannot dim the ridiculousness of the sight, in my mind, of a Rolls driver with his cigar stuck in his mouth the wrong way. Laugh then, or still smile years later, it's a great tonic.

A laugh can also carry a great philosophy. Once, a knock-out priest asked me to give a talk on religion in relation to human beings. Nothing out of the ordinary for me, except the situation. It was to be for nuns during retreat, in a convent. (Explanations here for the sake of the non-faithful. A retreat, in most of the pacifist religions, is when a collection of the faithful literally shut themselves away, usually for a few days, for contemplation.) Now, the idea of a supposedly raving pop man going into a convent during retreat is about equal to a nun paying to go into a stripclub. The priest who fixed this unlikely religious confrontation was a great and sincere character. The Mother Superior, aghast at such an idea, promptly took off for the day. So I arrived among these lovely ladies and talked of this and that.

At question time, a very important time during my talks, one of the nuns asked me, 'Why do the girls I teach not think very much of us?'

'Why do you think they don't?' is my question.

'Well,' says the nun, 'they laugh at us behind our backs.'

So I tell all the nuns, 'Look, people make jokes about George Washington and his cherry tree. Now it's not nice to joke about dead people but he's been dead years so it's reasonable taste. No one yet jokes about President Kennedy, but only because he hasn't been dead long enough yet. For all I know, even now visiting comedians in Dallas might just drop a clever ad lib about him. People laugh at me, anyone who gets a bucket of whitewash on their heads or slips on a banana. For years in seaside towns like Blackpool there've been funhouses where everybody gets a laugh at everyone else's expense, with funny mirrors, air jets that blow skirts up and suchlike—so, tell me why you should be so different from all the rest of the world that no one should ever laugh at you?'

I got a standing ovation for that one and then went on to tell them the old joke. 'What is it that goes black, white, black, white, black, white?' 'Don't know,' they said. 'A nun rolling down a hill.' So they all laughed at themselves and felt a lot better for it.

Laughing at people is still in doubtful taste and sometimes we get what we deserve. Some years ago, when portable battery-operated record players were a novelty, I got a great idea. Working in my dance hall of the time was a great character of a nightwatchman. Always full of fun, he was an ideal victim for my plot. There was at that time a horror-type rock record that had a ninety second intro of a door creaking open, rattling chairs and a long loud scream. Creeping back into the dance hall about 2 a.m., I go up on the balcony with my portable player. Turning up the volume I play the intro at full blast. The effect in the empty, silent dance hall was electric. A hoarse cry of fear came from below and there was much dropping of brushes and dustpans by my nightwatchman pal. I escaped from the balcony, made off on to the roof outside, stuck the speaker through a ventilator shaft and let go with the creaks, chains and screams.

Again my nightwatchman shot a foot into the air. I was rolling about with delight. An encore was definitely needed so I slid back into the hall. Now what I didn't know was that, just by chance patrolling outside, on foot, were two local coppers. Fearing a murder at least they had rushed into the dance hall. Heartened by their presence my victim suddenly became a lion. Seizing a sweeping brush he flew round the dance hall looking for either dead bodies or the murderer. We chanced on each other in the gloom of a passage and it was my turn to be terrified. So I turned tail and fled. Still killing myself with laughing I adopted a similar gait to the Hunchback of Notre Dame's. Hotly pursued and with tables turned I come to a locked door with no time to find the key. In an effort to frighten him back I put my overcoat over my head and shouted 'Booo!' For this I received a crack on the head that nearly put me right out. Down on the floor I go and collect a hammering off the brush end that nearly broke every bone in my body. My lion-hearted night man rushed off to fetch the two bobbies and more dead than alive I climb to my feet, find the key on my bunch and escape through the door, locking it behind and carrying what was left of my record player, smashed beyond repair.

The pay off really paid me off. Round the block in double quick time, a comb of the hair, and sweep in as the manager. Aching in every bone as well. The lurid description of the night's event, the pursuit, battering and final complete disappearance of this horrendous creature through a still locked door, 'See it for yourself Mr Savile', was all too much and I start laughing again. This strange reaction in no way surprises my night man as he is previously convinced that I am potty anyway. The coppers are mystified and prowl around ceaselessly.

Suddenly I am stiff with terror. My nightwatchman turns his eyes up and collapses on the floor. It has proved too much for him. Boy, I sweat in blocks. There is much first aid and loosening of collars. Round he comes, a bit shaky, and I have to send him home by taxi. This leaves me, you guess it, doing nightwatchman duties plus all his sweeping up that he didn't do.

Lucky escapes figure prominently in my apparently never-ending fun, money and health life. On one dance hall occa-

sion five young ladies came to me asking if they could stay
with me for the night as they had missed their bus home.
A somewhat strange request as it was only 8 p.m. and their
last bus didn't go till midnight. So after the dance we all
finish up back at my place. The fact that they all produced
nighties and toothbrushes caused me to marvel momentarily
at the completeness of ladies' handbags. (As it was Saturday
night it could have been premeditated but girls are not like
that surely.) After much running about the house, prep-
aration, girl talk and continuous idiot laughing we all collapsed in a heap and fell asleep.

Came morning with clear blue skies and sparkling sun.
Such ingredients make me sniff for the moors and mountains
so off I go on the bike leaving five females in a scene remi-
niscent of—right—the St Valentine's Day massacre. For
safety's sake I had brought a male minder just in case and
he was unconscious in the back room. Enter the dragon, or
as it happens, two, about 11 a.m. Two fire-breathing mothers
looking for disappeared daughters hammer on the front
door. Leaping into instant life as only daughters caught in
the act can, the girls fall downstairs full of explanation and
excuse. Such chat is carried by such girls, apparently, just
like their nighties and toothbrushes.

'Jimmy is away for the weekend and has kindly lent us the
house,' they lie.

'He is upstairs asleep,' holler the mums, 'for is it not a well
known local fact that he is dead to the world before midday?'

And up the stairs they rush like Customs and Excise men
about to do a rummage. The girls do a joint swoon at the
prospect of finding my sleep-sodden minder in bed. But no.
Down come the mollified mothers content that the house
harbours no daughter-consuming men.

'How kind of Mr Savile to lend you his house for the
weekend,' they cry. 'Make sure that thou dost clean it up well
and leave not piles of girl junk about like you do at home.'

167

And off they go, loud in my praises and beating their breasts at having thought ill of me.

But where is my big meaty minder? Why, in the wardrobe of course, for I train my men well and, to date, we have not been found out. Which, after all, is the eleventh commandment, is it not.

ABOUT THIS BOOK

Some people write books and some books write people. That's a typical left-handed Savilism. What it means is that this one simply wrote itself, using me, several pens and about eight cheap exercise books. It turned out to be one of the most pleasant jobs of my queer career.

I hasten to add that it was anything but an ego trip. Actually, some five years ago a book firm offered me much loot to write my life story. Such recognition is about equivalent to being elected Lord Mayor, and very gratifying if you like that sort of thing. I declined the invite for various reasons like I didn't need, therefore want, the money, plus putting one's life story up for cash seemed a dead liberty or incredibly big-headed. So why did I finish up doing it?

Well, one day a chap phoned me and said, 'There are so many stories about you on newspaper files that I'm doing your life story. If you help me I'll work you a few quid.'

Now that was a bit of a liberty plus there was another important factor. All sorts of stories circulate about people like me, in showbiz. A lot of them gently incorrect. For instance, I've never had a pink nor a purple Rolls but can't count the number of people who've seen me in one. The number of schools I went to is considerable, according to people who swear they were at the same one.

One day I was sitting on a kerb, halfway through a training session on the bike, and talking to a girl. Up comes a middle-aged guy.

'Hello Jim,' says he, 'haven't seen you for ages.'

'No,' says I to this total stranger, 'you look well.'

'By heck,' says the stranger, 'it's a long time since I used to carry you from the pub and you slept it off on our settee.'

'It sure is,' says I.

Off goes my new pal, well pleased at the meeting.

'Hey,' says the girl, 'I thought you didn't drink.'

'So, I don't,' says I.

'What was all that about you being boozed on his settee?' asked the puzzled chick.

'Well,' I explain, 'it's easier to agree than claim I've never seen him before.'

And so the stories circulate.

Therefore if someone who doesn't know you is going to write all about your life it figures that he's going to get it all wrong. At least wrong enough to make sure you spend the rest of your life explaining incorrectitudes. Even reporters with tape-recorders can make mistakes. On one taped interview, I mentioned I was entertainments officer at Stoke Mandeville Hospital. In the paper later this had been phonetically mistaken as 'Stoke Mental Hospital'. There was much phoning in that area to find the place that was keeping my employment so secret!

Plus I copped the gentle needle that I had lived my life and someone else was going to collect. So I let it be known, diffidently, that my autobiography was available. The result terrified me: or should I say the responsibility that went with the result. Dignified publishers descended into the pit of the pop world and talked about large chunks of money for large chunks of words. After agreeing terms I was faced with all sorts of decisions.

As Nat King Cole told me, 'Records were made to sell, and that's that.' Therefore books should be made to sell. From the printers to the papermakers, they all have families to keep, and if I elect to write a book I have to take the responsibility for all their success. Now there's all sorts of angles one can use to actually sell things. For instance, sexy books seem to get big sales so, as there has been much crumpet in my life, do I fill my book with stories like how I 'enjoyed' a young lady in the corridor of a train in broad daylight? Secretly but successfully. Impossible act you say? don't you believe it. Now tales like that might get sales but I didn't feel that was right. Not that I would keep such murky moments secret because of what people might think of me. It's human nature to want to be thought well of, otherwise we'd never bother to wash or shave, but a thing I always said to my disc jockeys was, 'Never try to make the public like you but make sure they can't dislike you.' So, in the middle of all this noxious responsibility at the outset of my authorship, I went, as always, back to my never-failing square one.

I went to Mass.

Explained to the Boss that I was lumbered with this not unpleasant task and would like some help so I could tread the right path, be honest but not fall for the easy way out. So off I went and started to write. Literally. Using no notes, diaries, newspaper clippings that the Duchess hoarded, or anything except paper and pen. Every word has been written in longhand by me. My fluid, fluent style enormously surprised the publishers—but not me, for writing stories, or composition as it was called then, was the only thing I excelled in at my elementary school.

Writing about one's life is personally fascinating. Providing one doesn't fall for the ever-present ego trip. Going back to the start and tracing slowly along through the years, I spent far more time daydreaming than writing. I can smell the exquisitely tobacco-flavoured handkerchiefs that I would seek for in my father's pockets and his measured tread down the hall. The whistle of the icy wind on top of Ben Nevis when I thought my time had really come. The Duchess nagging me about eating something and her innocent but impossible accounts of things I never did. Again I smell the kerosene from the jets of the Phantom fighter that came looking for me on top of the Struie pass, in Invernesshire: so low did he come on top of this super moorland, perhaps thirty feet, waggled his wings, stood the aircraft on its backside, and took off with the Dante's Inferno of all sound and smoke, completely blowing me into the ditch. The thrill of the first award I ever won, and the equal thrill of the hundredth! All these things make writing about one's life a time-consuming event.

I nearly stopped halfway through. All because I lost an exercise book in which I'd written about 4,000 words. It would have been a mental impossibility to re-write all that and a psychological impossibility to proceed after such an amputation. All my places were blitzed, down to pulling sundry carpets up. Beds and blankets were taken and shaken.

Friends rushed about eager to help and uncovered hoards of forgotten everything except the damn book. I found it down the back of the seat in my mini van.

The Good Lord never welcomed His lost lamb back with more enthusiasm, and the midnight scraping and scratching of the flying pen restarted. It occurs to me that working from memory, at leisure and with only the wall opposite providing any help (I rest my eyeballs on it), I could miss some stories. This could be, but only because of me being ruthless at not using what's called 'journalistic padding'. That is when you use the same sorts of stories in different ways so as to make up the necessary wordage.

One of my major difficulties was, of course, conscience. For instance, if a young lady had found me not unattractive and presented me with her all, it would not be the done thing to publish her story accompanied by her name and address and phone number. There are those business friends around who would laugh loud and long and would tell you that, in that case, this chronicle would finish up a cross between the London phone book series and the Guinness Book of Records. They would say that but I wouldn't.

Actually I've always fancied being an author 'cos it's the only job one could do from one's bed. I remember once, after an interminable flight over the North Pole, climbing out of the plane in Los Angeles. On board with me had been Cilla, Gerry and the Pacemakers and other fun people from Brian Epstein's incredible pop team. They were going on to Australia and as I watched them off I thought Cor, what a long way to go to earn a living. So to wake up, not have to get up and earn a living, surely is the greatest ever.

Also there is the thrill of the empty page. You start at the top and what will you do. Will you make people laugh by telling them the story of trying to get a friend some publicity?

He had just taken a pub so I volunteered to get his place in the paper by carrying a barrel of beer round the outside, on my back. The weight was incredible and how I managed it God alone knows. The sequel was that the strain actually interfered with my love life for nearly two weeks, and girls, several, fell into two categories. Half rushed off to improve their technique and the other half were convinced I was homosexual (which I'm not, as it happens).

Or, with the empty page shall I take a leaf from life and tell you of a simple hospital thing that actually tore me to pieces inside. Two girls I knew, patients both. Their complaint was one of the touch and go killers. I used to threaten enthusiastic mayhem to their honour, if I ever got chance. We had a fine thing going. Off I went to do the end-to-end walk and reappeared on the wards a month later.

Girl no. 1 is delighted to see me back and there is much story telling. After half an hour I turn to leave.

'Oi,' says I as an afterthought, 'where's your pal?'

'Oh,' says girl no. 1 coming back to reality, 'she died.'

This caught me a low blow. 'She didn't!' says I, feeling suddenly bad.

Girl no. 1 mistakes my emotion and thinks I'm annoyed with her pal for not waiting for me. 'She didn't want to,' she explains in a small voice, 'at least not until you got back from the walk.'

I swear I broke to pieces inside at that moment. Two teenage girls, who should be out and about, not wanting to die just yet. The sun shines outside, the cars bustle about and I get caught unawares by the innocent remark of a dying teenager. For she died some weeks later. I was there, this time, and yet once more did the disc of darkness inch slowly across the sunshine of my life. Feelings make life, or break it. Or cheer it or chill it.

So you see what I mean about the thrill of the empty page. I can't paint but I enjoy conjuring up pictures out of words.

The book has been a ball. I really hope you like it for I would really like people to know, enjoy and love Uncle Sid, the Duchess and all the others that I can't wait to see again, up in Boss Country.

'And so to bed' is a phrase as famous as my opening one, 'Don't call us, we'll call you.' But to bed it must be, for the story of my travels to date. The publishers cry 'Know thee not, Jim lad, that there is a world shortage of paper and shouldst thou write much more every tree must be felled for the BOOK.' Far be it that I should help to render our planet bald and treeless, like the Chang Tang Highlands, in Tibet. Now you didn't know I knew anything about that country did you? Well I do, and lots more that I haven't been able to fit in here.

Rumour has it that in certain parts of Polynesia there is a custom as follows. Should a virile Polynesian gentleman be walking through the forests of that area and by chance happen upon a young lady coming t'other way, he throws at her a small stone or fruit. If she should playfully cast it back he can hoist her speedily behind a local bush and give her a local anaesthetic. Such habits and customs I have not found in my native Yorkshire, indeed such jolly goings on are

174

labelled evil and rewarded with several months in the pokey. I must see these admirable Polynesians and, if it all be true, get them to join the Common Market. Why should they have it all?

Looking at this world of ours there are things to do that could keep a man busy for several hundred years.

So let us be off to attend to our affairs. For those lucky ones who will stay home with the wife and kids, I salute you and envy you more than you think. For me, the traveller, I will be off over the hill and bring you back stories and souvenirs from the other side of life. That great President of the U.S. of A., John F. Kennedy, was shot whilst on his way to make a speech in Dallas, Texas. The speech was never really published but I saw it and was knocked out by the text he was going to use.

For if the Lord guardeth not the sleeping city,
    The watchman waketh in vain.

And that's about it folks. We can all do good things on our own, but great things when we enjoy Good Company Of. So, God be with you all.

P.S. I hope He really *does* take it easy on sinners!!

P.P.S. As it 'appens!

LOVE IS AN UPHILL THING

Now then. Here we go with a brand new section. I re-named this paperback edition *Love is an Uphill Thing* because I wanted to call the original hardback that, but changed my mind and used one of my accidental catch-phrases, *As it Happens*.

Love is an Uphill Thing is a very apt line in most of our lives today. Whatever we would want to love, like, other people, or things, it's an uphill fight to reach it. The uphill bit can be fun and it's super when we get to the top, but you must have noticed how difficult it can be to get what you want.

This autobiography was intended as a sort of handbook and catalogue of stories that might even help some individual who, like me, never made the grade, academically speaking, but could still climb up the hill of life on the outside.

My love of life has been an uphill thing, sure enough, but great fun also.

The thing that really bugs me about life is the question of why are some of us so lucky and others so devoid of it. It really doesn't do for us mortals to think about it too much because you can get very down in the dumps on behalf of all the millions of unlucky people there are in the world. So let's cheer up with a couple of stories from me about two widely different places.

The House of Commons, and a mortuary. In both cases I was completely innocent of any villainy but, as usual, picked up the blame.

The scene is the terrace at the House of Commons. Assembled there are a goodly number of MPs and Ministers. They are entertaining some two hundred newspaper, radio and TV journalists.

Being teetotal doesn't exactly make one a cheerleader on such occasions and I was drinking a cup of tea, made specially by one of the ever friendly waitresses, when a group of guests wandered over for a chat. One of the young ladies of the party was very dolly and had an unusually large chest area. It being a warm evening and a low dress, her bosoms appeared to be trying to come up for some fresh air. Suddenly a terrible thing happened. One of the men struck a match to light a cigarette. The burning matchhead snapped off, flew in the air, and, fizzing like one of Guy Fawkes' fireworks, fell fair and square down her cleavage!

Her first scream would have caused Alfred Hitchcock to nod and say 'OK boys, that's a take'. Her second scream, much louder and with tightly closed eyes, was the pure stuff of pain in sensitive areas. Now, only three people had seen the disappearing match trick. Her, me, and he who had struck. He-who-had-struck was now standing there stricken, with a duff matchstick in his hand and his mouth open. No assistance could be expected from that quarter. Something had to be done so I seized her lower bristol area hoping it would smother the burning sulpher. Her third scream was a mixture of 'Jesus Christ'! for the pain 'You stupid clumsy sod!' for her luckless companion and 'Watch what your doing down there' for me. It was the final scream of the trilogy that drew the attention of most of the Terrace. All they saw was me, reefing the buxom wench and all presumed I'd suddenly gone mad. Amongst various cries of conjecture was a classic from one member of the House who exclaimed 'Good Lord, he's got her by the tits!' All was eventually sorted out but as is usual vastly misunderstood by most.

Another case of complete misunderstanding was in a hospital mortuary. It is a hospital porter's task to take the lately deceased from the ward to a temporary resting place in the mortuary. This is a serious job and most porters think of it as an honour that such a dignified task should be theirs. Now death has always interested me and during my voluntary hospital hours I have spent much time in various mortuaries reflecting on the insoluble questions that death poses. It was while visiting a nearby hospital that the following chain of disastrous events took place. The deceased, as is usual, are comfortably accommodated in an area which takes up one end of the mortuary and is kept cool by an ordinary fridge system.

The motor on this particular unit had broken down. It was also housed inside, with the occupants, and therefore was not an electrician's dream of an ideal workplace. The hospital electrician was away ill so a man had been summoned, privately, from the village.

'Ha,' said he when told the task, 'not likely.'

'It can only be a small job,' said the Head Porter, 'and see, Jimmy's here, he'll go with you.'

'I've nothing against dead bodies,' quoth the sparks, 'it's just that I don't want to get inside with them.'

He eventually conceded to the task and off we went. It was a Saturday afternoon in the summer and all the mortuary staff were off duty. To ease his qualms I left the outside door wide open into the corridor. In the fridge room, if you can picture one wall made up of ten full length doors, and inside the first door is the cooling unit.

Anticipating his objections I had already nipped inside and taken out the light bulbs so he couldn't even see what occupants there were. Plonking a chair in the middle of the floor I settle down with a cigar and the electrician peers inside, suspiciously, with his torch. After several hums and ha's he squeezes inside and says,

'I don't like this job one little bit'.

'Salright,' says I, 'actually I often come here for a crafty smoke.'

'You're welcome to it,' says my jumpy pal as he fiddles

with the motor. It was just then it all happened. Into the fridge room on rubber sole shoes comes a young porter. He had seen the outside door open and smelling my cigar, presumed, and obviously so, that I had nicked in for a sit down out of the way. His silent arrival nearly made me swallow my cigar, but then, sweet horror, seeing the door open wherein they kept the bodies, he slammed it shut.

A muffled cry of terror came from within. Several things happened at once.

It stands to reason that the unfortunate electrician has taken an immediate and vociferous dislike to suddenly being walled up with the dead. It also stands to reason that my porter pal will expect nothing but a decent silence from the various deceased and upon hearing a hoarse cry from the inside, therefore the wrong side, was so freaked that he collapsed to the floor.

I now had for company two completely freaked human beings and several lately departed ones. In a flash I had the fridge door open and an apparition of an electrician sprang out. A perfectly natural supposition on his part was that the shape on the floor was yet another client. Pausing not in his stride, and making a sound which is spelt 'aarrghhh' he fled the room, the hospital, and I have not seen him to this day.

The cause of all the trouble, albeit innocent, the porter on the floor, had (a) not known there was a live electrician in the fridge and (b) seen something spring out and rush off, therefore presumed that (a) someone had wrongly been buried alive or (b) had returned from the dead. As it happens I was beginning to wish that I'd stayed at home as well.

Needless to say that when all got calmed down there was a strong body of opinion that it was all down to me. As another porter put it, 'Things like that just don't happen when he's not here so it's got to be him.'

Working in a mortuary bothers me not at all because it's

the last stop before heaven so that can't be bad can it.

What does keep me in a constant state of the shakes is something like this.

Years ago, before I was well known, a young lady chanced across my path one afternoon.

'Come home with me,' she says.

Her house was one of those little north country ones that the front door opens straight into the living room.

'Are your parents at work?' says I.

'My husband is,' says she of the free afternoon indicating that I should sit with her on the settee.

It had never occurred to me that she could be married. Suddenly heavy footsteps clomped up to the door—my heart stopped—and the feet went clomping off down the street.

'Don't be silly,' she says 'people walk past all day and half the night.'

Not five minutes had we been sat down, a dozen people had walked past, giving me a heart attack, when, one set of feet didn't go past, but stopped, banged the door open, and walked in.

It was her mother!

'Oh,' said the lady, 'sorry.'

I sat there like a frightened rabbit. 'Want to borrow some flour for your Dad's Yorkshire pudding,' says Mam. The girl jumps up all of a twitter and produces a brown paper bag half full of flour. Mam stops looking suspiciously at me and looks suspiciously at the flour. 'Is it plain or self raising?' she queries.

For some reason the girl has been affected by my nerves and can't speak. Even then, good in an emergency, I leap up, dip a finger in the flour, taste it and pronounce 'Plain'.

It could have been cement for all I knew or cared.

Off goes Mam and off I go ten seconds later, faint at being free.

Two weeks later I see the girl in town.

'My Mam will never forget you. It was self-raising flour and she finished up with a Yorkshire pudding the same shape as the inside of the oven!'

And of course it had to happen, someone threatened to shoot me. Now there's a situation that takes some coping with. It's easy to understand that when with regular TV and radio series and a column in a Sunday paper you finish up with 45,000,000 people as a weekly audience, such a vast audience has to contain one or two cranks. But you can never tell if a crank is for real. It all started off at two o'clock one morning. I'd been at Broadmoor Hospital all day, organising for a forthcoming Country and Western show. In the office I share with the transport manager I have a private phone that I pay for. It starts to ring. I pick it up thinking it must be a wrong number at that time of night, but it's the duty officer at the B.B.C.

'Thank goodness I've caught you Mr. Savile,' says that gentleman. 'We've just had a phone call threatening your life if we don't pay a sum of money.' Brave or not, such an announcement knocks you for a six at first. This was December '74 when hijacking and shooting was going on all over the world. So we make a hurried arrangement for the police to pick me up at the London end of the M4, for a conference.

'It's got to be a crank,' I say when we meet up. 'Who on earth would want to knock me off?'

'This is the year of the crank,' says the law, 'and we can't take a chance.'

For the next three weeks I lived a most bizarre life. Surrounded by armed men, sometimes two, sometimes five, things got very exciting.

The first night was a hoot.

As I was preparing for bed, with two gun toting bodyguards downstairs in the foyer, I decided on a personal survival routine. My Royal Marine Commando dagger was placed by the pillow and, in case of unwonted attack I would seize the blade, roll off the bed, and come up fighting. Except it didn't quite work like that. I'd been asleep about an hour, it was pitch dark, and there came an almighty commotion at my door. Ding dong ding dong on the bell plus a great loud hammering. Frightened out of my wits I jump out of bed, starkers, and do a war dance of terror on the carpet. Forgetting all about the dagger and survival bit, fling the front door open and see an out of breath uniformed policeman.

'Thank God, you're all right,' says he and rushes off down the passage.

Apparently by an amazing coincidence some small-time burglar had chosen that night of all nights to try to rob one of the flats in my block.

No small-time burglar ever had such a big-time reception. By the next morning my nerves were sticking a foot out of my skin and the slightest unusual sound caused me to take off. The first job next day was a children's party which was to be recorded for a broadcast. Surrounded by three armed plainclothes men, we had just arrived, at the Aeolian Hall in London and were set upon by all the kids. After half an hour, and just about tea and buns time, there was a deafening bang just behind my head. Both my feet took off the floor. 'Ha ha,' said a small voice, 'that frightened you didn't it.' For it was one of the little kids with an oversize balloon and a pin, right behind us four grown-ups as a joke. Such a joke at such a time.

After ten days that felt like ten years it was Christmas and I sneaked off to Scarborough where nobody would dream of shooting anybody and by New Year all had calmed down. A death threat is like a bomb warning, ninety-nine times out of a hundred it's a hoax, but you have to take a reasonable precaution. The big thing was keeping it out of the papers, which we did, because publicity doesn't half please the loonies that cause the trouble.

On a much more pleasant note was a super party at Buckingham Palace. It was the first of a new kind of party given by the Queen and Prince Philip. All the guests were invited to arrive at ten o'clock at night. So I took my pyjamas and toothbrush just in case it turned into an all nighter. Almost the entire royal family was there plus dukes, duchesses, lords, ladies, the Prime Minister, half his Cabinet and so many people that it was not far short of a Coronation guest list. For me it was a splendid night. My highspot was while talking to the Duchess of Kent she came over all funny like nearly fainting. There was only the two of us, and she puts a hand to her head and says the Duchess equivalent of 'Cor I don't half feel a bit off.'

She didn't actually say that because when an ex-coalminer is face to face with a swaying Duchess, and top flight beautiful at that, all I remember is copping her round the waist and plonking her down on an adjacent royal sofa. I give her some of my lemonade and search furiously in my mind for the Royal equivalent of 'How about a cool off outside?' No chance, I am struck dumb with a bad case of love at first sight. After a while she feels better and goes off. Up comes the Duke of Edinburgh—'I hear you've just saved the Duchess of Kent's life,' says he,

'Who wouldn't?' I reply.

'And,' says Prince Philip, 'I hear you're going to be the last out tonight.' What he meant was this. With such a glittering team in attendance, and determined not to miss a thing, I'd mentioned to one of the Palace minders that I was definitely sticking it out to the death. And didn't I just do that. At three a.m., after a quick tour of the state rooms to make sure no one was lurking in a corner I go down to the front door.

'Have they all gone?' I ask the door team.

'When you go Jimmy,' says the head man, 'we lock the door.'

With a flourish I summon my twenty-eight-foot motor caravan, which has great difficulty in getting in under the arch, and off I go into sleeping London town after a most splendid evening.

And so dear friend we must press on to pastures new. Telling stories about my past is a strange thing for me because I am a hundred per cent future man. By that I mean that normally tomorrow is a big day for me. I would be the last person to suggest how other people should live but I do feel that if more people looked to the future instead of keeping alive the sins of the past, then more people could live a better life. Not that we shouldn't honour the dead, like Armistice day, of course we should. But we should try and not rush off to add more dead bodies to the pile.

Hark at me trying to make the world a better place to live in. But, we've all got to keep trying, haven't we?

Cheer up folks, tomorrow could be a big day for you.

God bless, once again,

Your friend,

SEND TODAY FOR THE
JIMMY SAVILE
PICTURE BOOK

25p. ONLY (Inclusive post and packing)

SAVILE'S TRAVELS WITH SUPER COLOUR PICS

Allow 21 days for delivery

PLEASE SEND ME........COPY/IES OF
THE JIMMY SAVILE PICTURE BOOK. I ENCLOSE
P.O./CHEQUE FOR.......PLEASE SEND TO:

NAME..

ADDRESS...

TOWN................................COUNTY.........................

LITTLE GIRL LOST:

Life and Hard Times of Judy Garland

AL DI ORIO

Judy Garland was the little girl lost – the child superstar who went into showbiz at the age of two and spent the rest of her life in front of the cameras. Judy was the waif whom the studios pepped up with one set of pills – and sent to sleep with another. She was the fabulous clown, the heart-rending singer, the tear-jerking straight actress whom the world took to its heart. And behind the public façade there were five marriages, breakdowns, heartbreaks and all the unhappiness of a little girl lost.

CORONET BOOKS

MARILYN

NORMAN MAILER

'The greatest achievement of Mailer's "novel biography"
is to have lent the flesh and pulse of fiction to the bones
of fact'

The Financial Times

'Mailer's exploration of a woman he never met is out-
rageous, overwritten and obscene. It is also brilliant,
exciting and sexy'

Vogue

'Compulsively readable'

Time Magazine

'He contrives to be courtier and lecher, lover and loved
one too'

The Sunday Times

CORONET BOOKS

HANCOCK

FREDDIE HANCOCK and DAVID NATHAN

For half an hour a week East Cheam was the centre of the world for a third of the nation's adult population. This childish, bombastic, indignant man, Anthony Aloysius St. John Hancock, had come to epitomize for millions the humour inherent in modern British life. The story of the real Anthony John Hancock is told here.

'A sensitive and skilled biography'
Barry Norman – *Evening News*

'I recommend the book as an honest account of his struggle, his triumph, his fall – a comedian with a touch of genius who had no enemy but himself'
Sunday Times

'This is a very good book indeed . . . a painful but useful analysis of why and how a gifted man destroyed himself'
Observer

'Entertaining and painful'

New Statesman

CORONET BOOKS

THE MOON'S A BALLOON

DAVID NIVEN

He has had one of the most varied lives, as well as one of the most spectacular film careers, of our time. Expelled from school, baptized by the Army and a London whore, David amusingly recounts his early adventures.

In America, where he was treated with endearing hospitality, he became a bootlegger, an organizer of Indoor Pony Races, and finally, through a piece of luck whi h would seem impossible if it were not true, he sailed his way into Hollywood studios and stardom.

His wartime experiences (he served with the legendary 'Phantom') are treated with characteristic modesty; and thereafter his return to Hollywood leads to a rather chequered career (including being fired by Goldwyn and winning an Oscar) and also to the greatest tragedy of his life – the death of his beautiful first wife.

This is one of the most amusing, outspoken, self-revealing, warm-hearted and touching autobiographies ever to be published.

'Delightfully funny. The charm permeates every page'
Evening Standard

CORONET BOOKS

RICHARD BURTON

JOHN COTTRELL and FERGUS CASHIN

HE WAS BORN RICHARD JENKINS – of a Welsh miner and a former barmaid in the black hills of South Wales

HE TOOK THE SURNAME BURTON – and became the most promising stage actor of his generation, with a voice of haunting beauty and a theatrical presence that was truly magnetic

HE BECAME ANTHONY AND FOUND HIS CLEOPATRA – in the world of films, of private planes, of beautiful women, of royal households

HE REMAINS THE FOREMOST ACTOR OF HIS TIME – never quite an Olivier or a Gielgud, never quite a Brando or a Steiger; but with a range of great width, with flamboyance and an intelligence that cannot be matched

'A fascinating rags-to-riches record of a talented man whose life looms almost as large as some of the heroic figures he's brought to the stage and screen'

Variety

CORONET BOOKS

SINATRA

ARNOLD SHAW

'Watch him at a recording session, jacket off, tie loosened, every sinew of his skinny frame straining in support of that incomparable voice . . .

'Observe him displaying that rakish, crew-cut charm, bowing to the ladies or tipping his hat to the crowd . . .

'And then you remember the punched noses, the brawls, the snarling temper, the truculence and the bulging bodyguards, and you wonder whether you're talking about the same fellow

'Obviously reservations will have to be made both in Heaven and Hell for this abrasive do-gooder born fifty-five years ago in Hoboken, New Jersey'
Donald Zec – *Daily Mirror*

Here is the first, truly great biography of Sinatra, of the man and the legend. As author Shaw describes the book

'This is not an etching, limned in acid; nor a portrait painted in oils; but a black-and-white drawing of a remarkable man and his world'

CORONET BOOKS

Autobiographies and Biographies
from Coronet

JOHN COTTRELL & FERGUS CASHIN
☐ 18785 9   Richard Burton   60p

NORMAN MAILER
☐ 18828 6   Marilyn (large Pictorial Format)   £2.50

DAVID NIVEN
☐ 15817 4   The Moon's a Balloon   60p

ARNOLD SHAW
☐ 12644 2   Sinatra   70p

AL DI ORIO
☐ 20747 7   LITTLE GIRL LOST: Life and Hard
                 Times of Judy Garland   95p

FREDDIE HANCOCK & DAVID NATHAN
☐ 20513 X   Hancock   60p

All these books are available at your local bookshop or newsagent, or can be ordered direct from the publisher. Just tick the titles you want and fill in the form below.

Prices and availability subject to change without notice.

....

CORONET BOOKS, P.O. Box 11, Falmouth, Cornwall.

Please send cheque or postal order, and allow the following for postage and packing:

U.K. – One book 18p plus 8p per copy for each additional book ordered, up to a maximum of 66p.

B.F.P.O. and EIRE – 18p for the first book plus 8p per copy for the next 6 books, thereafter 3p per book.

OTHER OVERSEAS CUSTOMERS – 20p for the first book and 10p per copy for each additional book.

Name...

Address...

....